Carole

It is such a pleasure
to have you as a
Recognition friend.
Keep Giving!

Ry Send

Praise for *GIVING the Real Recognition Way*
By Roy Saunderson

"Roy's book 'GIVING the Real Recognition Way' is a refreshing reminder of how important it is to acknowledge everyone around us." - **Douglas Tapp**, Vice President, Total Rewards, H&R Block Inc.

"For employers and managers, Roy Saunderson's 'GIVING' delivers more value than the same-named bestselling book by President Bill Clinton." - **Jay Whitehead**, President & Publisher of Crossing Media, HRO Today, HRO Europe, CRO, & FAO Today Magazines.

"'Giving the Real Recognition Way' provides People Managers with invaluable tips to engage their workforce to perform at an optimal level. Whether you manage a sales, service or support department, the tips and advice Roy delivers will benefit all and will advance the development of your high performing teams." - **Steve Richardson**, Manager, Recognition Programs, RBC.

"A positive and practical book for all managers to guide them in focusing on their people and using principles for giving effective recognition." - **Gordon J. Feeney**, Chairman of the Board, Rideau Recognition Solutions.

Also by the author

101 WAYS TO GIVE EVERYDAY REAL RECOGNITION

HOW TO FOCUS ON SUCCESS

GIVING
THE
REAL RECOGNITION™
WAY

**Employers' and Managers' Must-Have
How-To Guidebook for Getting Better
Results from Employees...
and Avoiding
Career-Crushing Mistakes**

ROY SAUNDERSON

RECOGNITION MANAGEMENT INSTITUTE

Real Recognition™ Series

RECOGNITION MANAGEMENT INSTITUTE
A Division of Rideau Recognition Solutions
473 Deslauriers
Montreal, Quebec H4N 1W2

Canadian Cataloguing-in-Publication Data

Saunderson, Roy,
Giving the Real Recognition™ Way: Employers' and Managers' Must-Have How-To Guidebook for Getting Better Results from Employees... and Avoiding Career-Crushing Mistakes

ISBN 978-0-9681767-2-6

1. Employee motivation. 2. Employee retention. I. Title: Giving the Real Recognition Way II. Saunderson, Roy, III. Title

For information about special discounts for bulk purchases, please contact Recognition Management Institute Special Sales at 877-336-9601 or e-mail your request to info@RealRecognition.com.

Cover design by Richard Lytwynuk
Printed by Finger Communications

This publication is printed on FSC certified 100% recycled paper.
The Forest Stewardship Council (FSC) is an international not-for-profit organization that supports socially and environmentally responsible forest management.

This book is dedicated to you, my readers.
May this book make your recognition giving
a little bit easier and a lot more "real."

CONTENTS

Section 1: 26 Secret Principles Behind
Giving the Real Recognition Way

Section 2: 35 Tips for Employers and Managers on Giving the Real Recognition Way

Section 3: 9 Career-Crushing Mistakes to Avoid

ACKNOWLEDGMENTS

I am very grateful to everyone who has helped make this book come to reality in such a short period of time. To say the least I want to express my gratitude to the mighty few who did all they could to get this book to the presses and back again.

In fact I feel much like Henry Van Dyke did when he said, "Gratitude is the inward feeling of kindness received. Thankfulness is the natural impulse to express that feeling. Thanksgiving is the following of that impulse." And so I am going to act on that impulse and express my thanks and gratitude to some special people who made things happen in record time and have been a support to me along the road to making Real Recognition™ a part of many organizations.

Thanks go out to:

- Peter Hart – for boldly stating the goal was going to be making the impossible possible, and supporting everyone involved in making it happen.
- Lonn Shulkin – for his invaluable help in managing the whole project right from the start after receiving the very first phone call one chilly winter evening.
- Jay Whitehead – the man behind generating the title, editing and making insightful editorial suggestions along the way.
- Irene Saunderson – my dear wife who has always stood behind me and helps make me all that I am becoming.
- Members of the Rideau Recognition Solutions team for their ongoing editing, project management, support, marketing and creativity including: Louise Mocellin Sa, Richard Lytwynuk, and Jennifer Lumba.
- My children Marjorie, Tisha, Andrew, Camille and Kyle and their respective spouses and children, for being the inspiration they are and reminding me what to be really thankful for in life.

- To my friends and colleagues at Recognition Professionals International who have invited me into the amazing world of employee recognition and allowed me to contribute my expertise whenever I can.
- For my friends with the Canadian Association of Professional Speakers who spurred me on when I first carved out my beginning focus on employee recognition.
- To my many clients who I have had the opportunity of working with and serving over several years, who have each raised good questions and allowed me to come up with reasonable answers to help them progress the cause of Giving the Real Recognition Way.

It is with even deeper gratitude that I express thanks to my parents, Marjorie and John Saunderson, who brought me into the world, and to my step mother Jean who took on the challenge of raising a typical two year old when she married my dad and who together steered me in the right direction even when it seemed I wasn't listening. The fruits of their labors are greatly appreciated.

Those simple words "thank you" can be the hardest words to say for some of us, but can mean the very most to those of us that need to hear it.

So for any I may have inadvertently missed, thanks to all of you who have influenced my life to make it what it is today and to all who have contributed to the experiences that have helped fill the pages of this book.

FOREWORD

"Last century, machines proved they could replace human muscle. This century, technologies are proving they can out perform human left brains – they can execute sequential, reductive, computational work better, faster, and more accurately than those with the highest IQ's".

Thomas L. Friedman
The World is Flat

Factor that growing reality into the continued growth of a global economy, the retirement of baby boomers, the rising pressure on educational improvement, and government resources stretched to their tolerable limits and we have either a prescription for doom or a scenario for opportunity.

For employers, one element is obvious and that is being able to attract and retain employee talent is going to be a major concern. Toward this end, Roy Saunderson, knowing that successful corporate and governmental managers will opt for opportunity, lays out the ingredients necessary to create an environment that *truly* recognizes employee value. This has now become a key management objective. No entity can afford the high costs of personnel turnover in this environment of world-wide competition for talent and experience.

Occasional flowers and bonbons will no longer suffice. Retention of quality talent is an art.

I remember several years ago a conversation with an executive of a large printing company who started out after high school working in the print shop and eventually rose to a vice presidency. He attributed a large part of his contribution to the company as being able to almost daily walk through the plant, greet people by their first name, and solicit their advice when a complicated work order came. His employees felt valued. Why? Because they were.

"Giving the Real Recognition Way" is a *must* read for all CEO's, managers, and business school students.

Respectfully,
Arne H. Carlson

INTRODUCTION

Employee recognition has long been shown to be one of the highest rank needs of employees. And interestingly enough the lack of recognition is one of the top reasons why people leave their places of work as determined from exit interviews.

It was this interest and curiosity about why giving people the recognition they deserved was so challenging for us to do, and so lacking, that led me to re-focus my speaking and consulting business. So in 1996, I founded the Recognition Management Institute, a consulting and training company. I had two goals for the Institute. First, was to be able to conduct behavioral research and consult with leading organizations on effective employee recognition practices. Second, was to educate leaders and managers on the importance of employee recognition and show them how to give it effectively through means of books, articles and by delivering my message through keynote presentations, educational seminars and other resource mediums.

Since then I have delivered workshops as well as keynote presentations across North America to the private and public sectors. I initially thought I was going to save the world for all employees by seeking out all of the low morale companies and organizations that ever existed. Then I would show them how to change things around for the better and they would all end up with happy and appreciative employees. Unfortunately that marketing strategy never worked!

The irony was the companies who sought out my services were always the ones who already had an existing reward and recognition program. You might ask yourself why there was this disconnect and why they even needed this expert's help?

More often than not the request for assistance followed the review of results from employee satisfaction surveys which indicated employees did not feel fully appreciated for the contributions they were making at work.

Then meeting with senior leaders and human resource professionals, I would naturally ask about their present recognition programs and practices that were in place and put forward clarifying questions to understand what was working well and assess why some things obviously were not.

During the initial stages of doing this work on employee recognition I began to ask corporate leaders whether what they were doing was actually "real recognition" or not. The use of these words tended to spark some interest in people and inevitably generated the question, "So what is this 'real recognition?'"

From then on I started to realize the importance of my choice of words and officially coined and adopted the term "Real Recognition™" into my lexicon. These two simple words have caught on with many people I have worked with and shown how to personally give "Real Recognition™" and how to implement it throughout their organizations.

After more than ten years of helping clients give "real recognition for real results," I have been given the opportunity to compile the many newsletter articles I have written into a series of books that will further help disseminate the information I have gained to an ever wider and far reaching audience.

This volume will give you some of the principles behind giving what hundreds of corporate clients and tens of thousands of employees know as "Real Recognition™." It will also show you some very creative and practical tips and techniques for giving the people you work with the recognition they deserve.

Read, re-read and apply all that you learn within these pages. I want to hear from the employees where you work talking about Giving the Real Recognition Way because of the results they delivered as a result of your appreciation, praise and recognition.

Get ready to get real results from Giving the Real Recognition Way!

Roy Saunderson

Section 1

26 Secret Principles Behind Giving the Real Recognition Way

1.

GETTING "REAL" ABOUT RECOGNITION

You are going to find throughout this book a strong emphasis on giving what I have termed as "Real" recognition. The kind of recognition that employees feel is genuine, sincere and meaningful. It tells them they are valued and respected.

Giving employee recognition and especially *Real Recognition*™ is making an impact on employee engagement as well.

The renowned Gallup Organization uses a recognition targeted question right in their *Gallup Q 12* assessment used to measure employee engagement. The question is simply, "In the last seven days, have you received recognition or praise for doing good work?"

From a commissioned study in 1998, Gallup concluded the following. Watch carefully the cause and effect flow here: profitability, productivity, and employee retention and customer satisfaction are linked to employee satisfaction.

Are you ready to understand what influences employee satisfaction? Their study revealed employees who receive recognition are much more likely to be extremely satisfied with their employer.

Their research showed the vast majority of employees receiving recognition or praise feel it motivates them to improve performance. This fact correlates with research I have conducted in the public sector where 92 percent of managers agreed or strongly agreed that recognition improves employee satisfaction (*Survey Findings of the Effectiveness of Employee*

Recognition in the Public Sector, Public Personnel Management, Vol. 33, No. 3, 2004).

So employee recognition strongly impacts scores on employee satisfaction, which in turn affects performance and motivation. The Gallup group further added that difference in the levels or degree of employee satisfaction is greatest when recognition and performance measurement are combined.

How does recognition affect employee engagement? Depending on the number of items or questions used in your engagement index, the level of effectiveness with recognition can have a smaller or greater impact on your scores.

However, from an employee perspective the degree of respect and value they feel for the contributions they make at work will significantly determine how engaged they are to give the discretionary effort for a company, their willingness to stay with the organization, or even recommend their company to family or friends as a good place to work.

A 2002 report from the Office of the BC Auditor General on *Building a Strong Work Environment in British Columbia's Public Service: A Key to Delivering Quality Service,* identified *"individual recognition"* as one of the top three factors for improving the levels of employee satisfaction and employee engagement the British Columbia public service.

Note it was "individual recognition" that was highlighted as a contributing factor. More often than not, this means face-to-face, relationship based Giving the Real Recognition Way.

Consider a further Gallup study conducted in 2000 which showed "most workers rate having a caring boss even higher than they value money or fringe benefits."

Now they interviewed 2 million employees at 700 companies to make that conclusion! They also discovered how long an employee stays with a company and how productive they are is determined by the relationship they have with their immediate supervisor.

Real Recognition™ is about relationships. Giving recognition the right way should become a critical strategy for both retaining great employees as well as focusing on successful performance and results.

WorldatWork, a major compensation, total rewards and benefits association, found non-cash rewards programs achieved three times the return on investment compared with cash-based programs.

A return on investment analysis validates employee recognition practices as a contributing practice to bottom-line business results like any other strategic initiative. One has to start with clear and measurable objectives being set around employee recognition. Then the gaining of employee feedback and satisfaction with recognition will be an essential add-on to the impact analysis of recognition and how it has assisted in making an engaged workforce.

CEOs and senior human resource leaders should demonstrate through reviewing available metrics the degree of impact Giving the Real Recognition Way is having on results and retention. In this way, the "I" in ROI is more than just about *investment* in programs, training or communications, it is also about the return made on each *individual* employed within the organization as well as the *intangible* measures of improvement such as satisfaction and engagement.

Always remember Giving the Real Recognition Way is one tool of many in the leadership and human resource arsenal to help keep your employees engaged in the workplace.

2.

YOU HAVE 48-HOURS TO GIVE

Too many people tell me it is so hard to get recognition happening in their organizations.

I am here to tell you that recognition giving improves when people improve giving recognition. Re-read that last statement and imprint it on your mind as a solid principle behind Giving the Real Recognition Way.

So I am going to share something that has most often been attributed to the motivational expert and speaker, Anthony Robbins. Now whether you agree with him or not, there are some behavioral and cognitive principles he espouses that are right on the money.

In order to acquire new habits and change negative behaviors, you must take massive action towards your new goal or changed behavior within the next 48-hours.

Remember, recognition giving improves when people improve giving recognition. It is as simple as that.

What action towards improving recognition will you make? You only have 48-hours to give after reading this chapter.

Go Get'em Giving Ideas

1. For individual goals make sure you are taking on something realistic and doable. It does not have to be out of your comfort zone. Just out of your seat!

2. Team and group goals must have total involvement from each member. No involvement, no commitment. Each person

has to be able to take on a simple action that is manageable for improving recognition practices in the workplace. The goal is short-term success to create momentum. A goal in motion creates more action.

3.

WHAT COUNTS MOST WITH
SERVICE AWARDS

Corporations recognize employee behaviors many ways, both formal and informal. Chief in the formal award is usually the long-term service award.

Some organizations create the customary five-year increment awards. Many public sector organizations have, for some reason, done the grand leap and actually start at 20 or 25 years.

Now there is some debate whether there is still any merit to long-term service awards. Especially so when the average length of time organizations can keep people these days hovers around 3.5 years.

Yet the demographics of a lot of companies and public sector organizations reveal an aging workforce that has expected recognition for time given on the job.

But let me share with you a secret principle employees tell me about in regards to long-term service awards.

No matter what the award, gift or event that is done for long-term service, it is the "execution," the delivery, the "how it's done," that counts the most. In other words giving service awards has to be done the Real Recognition™ way.

Recognition Horror Stories

Let's first look at how *not* doing it the Real Recognition™ way negatively affects people. A few horror stories from the mouths of some actual employees will explain my point:

- Imagine your 25-years of service gift of a clock ending up on your desk in the original packing box from the shipping department, opened, with packing material hanging out.

- Or how about receiving your 25-years service certificate arrive in the brown, ugly, worn out inter-office courier bag

- Then there is the 25-years of service employee who was invited out to lunch with their spouse and received a lovely award – only to be left to pay the bill for their own and their spouse's meal.

- For another employee the 25-year anniversary date goes right on by with their manager not even saying a word.

Do you get the picture?

Real Recognition Way Principles

So let's create some shared principles and basic strategies for dealing with long-term service awards correctly and doing it the Real Recognition™ way:

1. Everyone really wants to be acknowledged for his or her contributions made over time.

2. The longer the length of service in number of years, the greater the expectation by the employee recipient for the special type of acknowledgement to be given.

3. Anniversaries of any kind are both a very personal experience as well as a shared event with others.

Go Get'em Giving Ideas

1. Whether through software reminder systems, written reminders or mental notation, REMEMBER the day of their service anniversary as well as honoring them at designated annual or scheduled corporate events.

2. Seek out ideas and information on expectations for celebrating length of service awards from older employees. Don't second-guess. It will only get you into trouble.

3. Personalize everything around long-term service awards and orchestrate everything to highlight each individual and their contributions.

4. Ask who they want to be present at ceremonies and invite them to come. Bring along a camera to capture the occasion!

For further guidance on giving service awards and gifts the Real Recognition™ way, read my article *What You Get Is Important, But How You Get It Sends A Message* at our website at **www.realrecognition.com/article2.htm**.

4.

E-MAILING THANKS FAST & RIGHT

Research by Christina Cavanagh, professor of management communications, now at the Rotman School of Management of the University of Toronto, indicates while e-mail may save time at work it can also cut into our productivity.

She found that 45 percent of the e-mail received by business executives could be ranked as "junk mail" – messages having "low" or "no relevance." With reference to the fact that many people are reading more than 60 e-mails a day, Cavanagh's research indicates this junk mail percentage adds up to a lot of wasted time sorting through unwanted e-mails.

Cavanagh completed her comprehensive study into the productivity of e-mail in the workplace and you can read the results and her insightful recommendations in her book, *"Managing Your E-mail: Thinking outside of the inbox"* (2003, published by Wiley, ISBN #: 0471457388). You can also visit her website at www.christinacavanagh.com.

E-mail as a Recognition Tool

So what about sending thanks and notes of congratulations using e-mail? Is it the right thing to do? What can make our e-mail acknowledgement come across better using the Real Recognition™ way?

Employees in the sales division of a major manufacturing company I worked with said they felt the e-mails they were receiving were only a knee-jerk reaction to performance results. Problem was they were not getting *any* face-to-face verbal recognition, just the e-mails. There was too much reliance on e-mail to make the recognition "real."

Doing recognition the Real Recognition™ way considers making any praise or acknowledgement as timely as possible. The beauty of e-mail is the ability to respond fast. I have sent a congratulatory e-mail out and received an unexpected acknowledgement back the same day. They really appreciated the message being sent.

Always remember to look for the principles behind the Real Recognition™ way. So when you hear something good about someone or they have achieved a significant outcome you have some choices in how you express your appreciation. You can go to them personally and praise them face-to-face. You can take the extra time and effort of writing them a personal handwritten note. Or you can dash off an e-mail in seconds and have them receive it within minutes of hearing about their action.

Another employee shared how they received an e-mail praising their work. The manager who sent it later came on the floor and spoke with the person but never brought anything up about the well-done task. This oversight negated the whole effect of the very good e-mail in the eyes of this employee.

Ann Coombs in her book, *"The Living Workplace"* (HarperCollins, 2001, or at www.thelivingworkplace.com) suggests e-mail can create other problems just because of our poor writing skills. Verbal feedback is obviously the best method, and as Coombs suggests "The physical voice is an instrument that permits the speaker to touch another's soul."(p.117)

Go Get'em Giving Ideas

1. Face-to face recognition will always be better perceived than any written or e-mail recognition. Though, the key is

using a mix of the different ways of recognizing. Use all available mediums and don't be dependent on just one way.

2. Cavanagh suggests using newspaper style efficiency in writing your e-mails. This will help guide you in e-mailing thanks and congratulations the Real Recognition™ way. Start with your subject heading capitalized with a catchy and succinct title. Put the most important reason why you're thanking or congratulating them right in the very first sentence. Then say how their actions benefited you or the organization. Tell them how it made a difference. Make this an e-mail worth reading amidst the flood in their inbox.

3. Never be afraid of recognition redundancy. If you send an e-mail to someone and then you end up seeing the person face-to-face later on, take time to verbally repeat the praise or acknowledgement you had sent them in writing. Twice said is twice valued. To ignore this is to lose the e-mail impact.

4. For something different on the e-mail scene, ask people how they feel about receiving electronic thank you cards. Some employees like them and some don't. Many companies are including their own repertoire of online e-Cards to send employees for various occasions and needs. Those who like receiving e-Cards will appreciate the time you took to select a fitting "card." Craft your own personal comments with care.

5.

CAN YOU BE SPECIFIC?

Can we get specific about recognition, please? This simple secret will make you a pro in giving thanks and praise the Real Recognition™ way.

Somehow the message about being specific has not gotten through to many people yet. Let me review with you what I call the Principle of Specificity. It goes like this: when specifying what is being recognized, you bring recollection of the action to the person's mind. When specifying why it made a difference, you give them purpose and add connection of emotion between people and the action completed.

Social scientist, Fred Luthans, from the University of Nebraska, identified the importance of being specific in his research on *"The Impact of Recognition on Employee Performance: Theory, Research and Practice."* Using the term "informative content" to describe specific feedback, he notes that effective recognition insists on specifics in order to have any value.

He further adds, "This detailed form or recognition not only conveys acknowledgement and genuine appreciation, but also information for reinforcing behavior that can lead to improved performance. Standardized phrases such as 'good job' have no such informative content that can lead to performance improvement; it becomes an 'empty reward,' not a positive reinforcer detailing how to improve performance."

So with giving everyday recognition the Real Recognition™ way I insist on people using the "Two-Part Specificity Rule" to make the secret difference.

1. First, tell the person specifically what it is you are recognizing them for, and…

2. Then tell them specifically how what they did made a difference to you personally, or to the customer and/or the organization as a whole.

Example: *"Thanks for getting this report done in such a timely fashion. I can't tell you enough how good I am going to look for having these numbers ready before the end of the month."*

Note how the expression of thanks specifically acknowledges the speed in which the report was completed and goes on to specifically state the impact this efficiency will have on the person's boss as well. You absolutely must use both to give the Real Recognition™ way.

What About Formal Recognition?

Look for the principles buried in these next few ideas. With formal award programs people need to know the specific categories they can be nominated for. Individuals should know the exact criteria they will be judged on and specifically how they will be evaluated. After the formal judging process people want to know how they scored either as a winner or as a nominee for possibly re-submitting for future award nomination opportunities.

There are a few organizations I have been talking to lately who are establishing giving out employee recognition certificates as nominated awards. It sounds like they are only giving general "ideas" to everyone as to when you can nominate someone. I have seen this kind of set up before and you get the exceptional minority making nominations because they understand recognition. Then there's the ordinary majority still wondering what they can nominate people for.

Quick aside here: be careful who you ask to be the evaluators of the award nominations. Some organizations I have seen used just senior management as the evaluators. I can't emphasize enough how important it is for you to also have some representative employees involved in the judging process. Getting them included will help increase participation because of the greater perceived level of fairness and integrity.

When you establish specific multiple category award options, like excellence in communications, or leadership, technology, innovation, teamwork, community service, heroic acts, etc., you immediately give "specific" cues that people can keep an eye open for. Then with the specific judging criteria and very often a numerical scoring process, nominated individuals can be judged fairly and know exactly where they stand once the judging has been completed.

Have I made myself specific enough on this? I know you got the message. To get others Giving the Real Recognition Way help pass this secret principle along to others for the benefit of all. Just be real specific!

Go Get'em Giving Ideas

1. Be real clear about *what* it is you are recognizing people for. You need to be able to tell the person on the street so they will understand and nod their head in approval.

2. So what? Tell the recipient *why* this act of recognition or award is being given. People get really motivated and excited when they know the "why" behind things. Let them know how they made a difference to you, the customer, and their department or to the company or organization served.

6.

WHERE'S THE GRATITUDE?

After our Christmas holidays are over, if you are like my household, we make time to write some thank you notes for the gifts we received from various relatives. This is an annual tradition and when more of the children were at home and younger we even had fun making the thank you cards we wrote in.

Now here are some interesting research findings carried out for the Society of American Florists to show the importance of those cards we write each year. Over half (52%) of Americans surveyed do not expect a thank you when they give a gift to someone.

Somehow we have lost the quality of gratitude. We need to be expressing gratitude the Real Recognition™ way.

However this research did reveal some great principles that are becoming lost in the workplace. Some of the insights suggested the most acceptable ways of thanking someone for a gift. Naturally, personal modes of communication were the highest ranked, as indicated below:

#1: In-person thank you (84% agree)
#2: Handwritten note (82% agree)
#3: Phone call (68% agree)
#4: Voicemail message (29% agree)
#5: E-mail message (27% agree)
#6: Faxed note (24% agree)

Notice when the degree of personal contact lessens, the lower the perceived level of acceptance with the type of communication used to express "thanks." Giving recognition the Real Recognition Way is all about relationships.

As you acquire business or whenever you receive a gift from a colleague or friend, make the time and write them a short handwritten thank you note. By the looks of the research they won't be expecting it and you'll be developing the lost art of gratitude. You'll be thanking them the Real Recognition™ way.

Just don't tell my children that their relatives are probably not expecting a thank you note!

Go Get'em Giving Ideas

1. Part of making Real Recognition™ giving a way of life is to make it a way of life… at home and at work. You have to get into the habit of sending thank you notes out to people for those wonderful gifts you receive throughout the year.

2. Now, while the in-person verbal thanks or written thank you are the best ways to say thank you for a gift or act, try mixing the type of recognition given especially when acknowledging the same person over time.

7.

RECOGNIZE THE DOING

The one thing I hear over and over again from employees at the organizations I have worked for, is "no one says thank you around here!" The way of giving Real Recognition™ has become a lost art in some places.

Employee satisfaction surveys conducted at many of these companies and organizations show employees love their jobs. What they don't know and *want* to know is whether their contributions on the job are appreciated.

So listen up on this secret principle that will make your recognition efforts stand out. Too many times managers and supervisors wait for the big job or project to be *completed* before acknowledging the work. Employees want to know along the way.

It's a simple recognition tip that will make a huge difference in people's lives. Recognize the *doing* and celebrate what's *done*.

Tell them while the work is progressing specifically how well they are doing and how it makes a difference to you and the company. When the project is completed that's when you can celebrate together. You can do this with refreshments or through an appropriate event or action.

Go Get'em Giving Ideas

1. Keep it fresh. BC Hydro executives once mandated themselves to give 15 percent of their time to being out listening to employees in order to correct negative perceptions employees had of them. You can prevent similar problems by

making time to do the walk-around. Be a keen observer of the workplace environment and actual work being done. Ask questions so you can understand the job at hand. Then you can make a genuine statement of appreciating the *doing* while it is still fresh!

2. Pass it along. Some managers are concerned they won't see their employees in action to be able to recognize the doing. Yet often a management team collectively will see direct reports from their peers doing great work. Pass along your observations to the respective manager and encourage them to give a second-hand compliment for the work being done.

8.

MEASURING THE RIGHT STUFF

From two similar presentations delivered in two different parts of the country, I obtained exactly the same results from surveying the respective audiences.

By using a list of 10 common barriers to giving Real Recognition™, the statement *"Finding the right measures for each person"* was by far the highest ranked barrier these particular groups found as getting in the way of giving people recognition.

Measuring performance has been the #1 rule of business success and has been associated with various methods of reward and compensation. I have long appreciated and used the following quote by a Thomas S. Monson which says, *"When performance is measured, performance improves. When performance is measured and reported, the rate of improvement accelerates."*

But do we have to measure everything? The right answer will identify you as a master of giving recognition the Real Recognition™ way.

The answer of course is "no!" Let's not make the lack of measures prevent us from giving sincere and genuine praise and acknowledgement for the contributions our employees make. Far too many employees take me aside when I am conducting organizational assessments and explain that all they want to receive are the two simple words "thank you!"

Measuring Right

Make sure you understand this principle. You can only measure goals that have quantifiable outcomes. Those goals and expectations must be known, and hopefully owned and originated by the employee.

For those things not directly quantifiable, there are qualitative outcomes such as living the corporate values and displaying behaviors and attributes consistent with those beliefs. These are observable actions of word or deed. In that sense they are also measurable.

What if you don't see these actions yourself? Better to give a second-hand compliment heard from someone else than give nothing at all.

There is no doubt from the audience surveys mentioned that I think we may be a little too preoccupied with only things we measure as the impetus for giving recognition.

Keep this simple principle in mind: *Performance reigns, but feelings rule.* Never ignore the value of saying thank you and giving appreciation for the person, just for who they are independent of any performance measures.

Go Get'em Giving Ideas

1. Follow the doctor's orders. When you go for a doctor's visit they always check the outside measures first, such as height and weight - quantitative. Those can be easily assessed and are hopefully constant. Any changes reveal a need for adjustments to be made. The doctor checks the inside by asking where something hurts or if any changes have occurred since your last visit – notice these are qualitative. So play doctor with your recognition measures.

2. Return and report back. No matter what measures you have available to you they still need you to interpret and clarify them. You can then determine if any course correction is necessary. To not act on a problem is to stick your head in the sand and this makes measuring a waste of time. Measures also allow you to give accountability reports in your management stewardship and help you with your recognition strategy planning. Measurement is the grand starting point of Giving the Real Recognition Way.

9.

FOCUS ON YOUR BEST

One of the things I am continually hearing on the issue of employee recognition, is that managers keep forgetting to say or show appreciation to their high performing employees. The reason given is because they are always dealing with issues from low performing employees. You know, putting out fires.

The only problem is high performing employees see this. They say to themselves it doesn't matter if you work your guts out to help the company, nobody notices. But create a problem around here and you get tons of attention. They deserve to be recognized the Real Recognition™ way.

If you lose out on this principle you will also lose the war on employee retention.

What do you do?

Organizational behavior research consistently shows in any group of people there are about 15 percent who are the movers and shakers – your high performers. At the other end of the bell curve are another 15 percent who are the low performers, the rebels. In the middle are the rest of the 70 to 80 percent who are the fence sitters. Half of them are passively "against" things and tipping over the line in the other direction is the other half who is passively "for" things.

Keep this secret principle top of mind, namely to focus on your best, your top performers. By concentrating and recognizing these stars they will pull everyone on the curve up towards them. The group who is passively for will be attracted in that direction. They want the same as the top performers.

You will even shift the scales on some of the fence sitters who are passively against.

You will *always* have a bottom 15 percent who will be working against you. Manage these people but *don't* focus on them. Give them feedback and coach them but *don't* give them any more time than your top performers.

You must focus on your strengths – your top performers – and you must manage your weaknesses – your poor performers.

Go Get'em Giving Ideas

1. Rotten apples. One rotten apple can ruin the whole barrel. Poor performers eat away at your very best people when no action is taken to correct their behaviors. They take away from the Real Recognition™ way. You probably have already seen it at places where you have worked. What happens is the best performers become less engaged and the motivation and enthusiasm starts to turn off.

So catch people doing what's right and stop people from doing what's wrong.

2. Meet with your top performers regularly and find ways to endorse their ideas. Find out what does turn the light on for them. You will more likely find out they want more responsibility, projects to take on, more challenging stuff and opportunities to do something innovative. Real Recognition™ does not have to be about things. It's about people first. When you do things right you will not have to motivate your high performers - just give them permission to do and then move out of the way!

10.

KEEPING THE TRADITION GOING

A cornerstone of Real Recognition™ is that award-giving must become a tradition that just keeps getting better and better every year. In the media business, annual rank-based awards such as the Fortune 500 or Forbes 400 are known as "numerology" tools, a sure-fire way to build reader engagement and advertiser loyalty.

CRO Magazine, the magazine for Corporate Responsibility Officers, the newest corporate function, publishes the 100 Best Corporate Citizens, a list that has appeared every year since 1989. The ranking is based on publicly-available data and covers corporate governance, compliance, sustainability and corporate social responsibility behaviors of Russell 1000 companies. The publisher has told me that companies often lobby hard to be ranked high. For example, the Chief Administrative Officer of the 2008 top-ranked company, Intel, told the publisher that the top spot has been in the company's sights for over eight years.

Intel has been on the list several times, and many companies including Cummins and Eaton, have been on the list every year since its first publication. Recipients and those who aspire to the award over the years have instilled major value in the 100 Best brand, a mark that adds significant value to the brands of those companies who received it. Recipients have profitably mixed ethical behaviors with their business practices—a tough act that certainly deserves recognition.

A Real Recognition™ principle is to steal a page from the media business and make your annual award-giving traditions ongoing by honoring all of your past recipients. What an honor roll that will be!

Go Get'em Giving Ideas

1. For Public View. Some awards such as the ethics award are good for displaying current and past recipients for both the recognition of the receiver and example setting for others to emulate. Develop a social standard for others to copy. Even design your own award to sponsor.

2. For Private Eyes Only. Not all awards would have meaning to the public. Make sure you communicate using your internal intranet, newsletters, staff meetings and award events to acknowledge recipients of nominated and earned awards. Add to it by noting past recipients and create your own honor guard!

11.

THREE VERY IMPORTANT FACTORS

After working with many corporations, government agencies and associations, I have certainly seen some common threads to what makes a successful recognition environment. In fact you will find them to be solid principles to guide your recognition practices.

These three very important factors that I present to clients for their own self-assessment is Values, Skills and Awareness. To be giving meaningful and effective recognition in the workplace all three need to be in place at a high functioning level. This is the stuff that makes the Real Recognition™ way a reality.

Values and Skills Alone

When Values and Skills are in place you have a "Could Do" mindset towards recognition. When Awareness is missing leaders are just not aware of the need or lack the insight of the importance of employee recognition. Listening to their own employees first and benchmarking by looking outside at successful organizations and best practices will be a good starting point to increasing awareness.

Just Values and Awareness

Now when Values and Awareness exist in any organization without the Skills component, they generally have a "Would Do" recognition attitude. They just lack the skills, the know how on how to give recognition the Real Recognition™ way. They believe in the importance of recognition, they are even aware of the need, but they just don't know how.

What about Skills and Awareness?

Skills and Awareness on a high score overlap to create a "Should Do" focus. Just the Values are absent. These organizations and their people know the need and even know how to do it. What's lacking are strong and articulated beliefs and values from leaders that recognition giving is the right thing to do.

The Need for All Three Factors

Values will always drive successful recognition initiatives. Awareness of the benefits and importance of recognition will give incentive to learn and to do. Skills provide the confidence and competence of what to do and how to give recognition effectively to employees. All three are essential for making the Real Recognition™ way a part of the recognition culture.

Just three essential factors for getting everyone committed in your organization to giving each other the kind of recognition they really want... Real Recognition™!

Go Get'em Giving Ideas

1. Better check how these three factors stack up in your organization. You can't be lopsided if you want a successful organization. An effective recognition strategy is driven and led by the values on the back of managers who are well skilled and aware of the importance of recognition giving.

12.

RECOGNITION BY COMMITTEE

You have probably heard the definition of a camel – a horse made by a committee!

With the de-layering of the workforce there is a trend to relegate employee recognition to a committee as well. I just hope we don't get too many camels in place of meaningful appreciation, praise and recognition.

Some committees are strictly made up of employee/associate folks and occasionally supervisors. They work their tails off acknowledging and organizing service anniversaries, seasonal celebrations, and just plain trying to make people feel good about what they do.

Other committees are more diverse with both employees and managers on board with a big picture focus. It is this mix of people that I am seeing which contributes to making recognition a success the Real Recognition™ way.

Legerdemain – Slight-of-Hand

When just employee level people are on the committees there is often a management kind of slight-of-hand, dumping it on contributing employees so managers don't have to do anything. Awareness does increase for a few managers, but slowly. You still get some managers leaving it all to the "recognition team." This tends to breed negativity in employees towards the team's efforts because of poor management example and commitment.

Seems as soon as you get managers on committees there is a more strategic approach to getting others in the organization involved. Perhaps the perception of having more clout with authority helps.

Learn this next important principle from an experience I had. One committee I worked with had followed a philosophical approach of developing a guiding purpose and a written mandate for recognition in the workplace. Instead of a committee mandate it's the entire organization's focus. Here's the principle: strategic thinking always wins over individual thinking.

No wonder they were able to get senior management support along with approval of planned management and committee member education, website development, and formal awards processes in place.

Go Get'em Giving Ideas

Making a successful recognition committee consists of:

- Ensuring a mix of managers and employees committed to making recognition happen.
- Senior leader support with a specific executive champion.
- Clear philosophical strategy statements of purpose and committee mandate.
- Strategic goals to be achieved by the organization and not *just* the recognition committee.
- Aligning recognition plans with achievement of corporate performance goals.
- Accountability to and from senior management on a regular basis.
- Regular communication through written word and events of what is happening with recognition initiatives.
- Establishing baseline measures to use as guides for benchmarking and ongoing evaluation and improvements.

Get rid of any "camels" in the making where you work. Ensure a successful recognition committee by following the simple suggestions and principles above.

13.

LET'S GET VISIBLE

Here's the irony.

Many organizations have recognition policies or programs already established. Yet when I talk to the managers and employees some don't even know anything about them and the rest are just plain not receiving any recognition even when they do exist.

If you don't know a recognition strategy exists and you can't see the recognition strategy in action, recognition just won't happen. A strategy is essential to making the Real Recognition™ way happen.

Apply this principle to combat these kinds of problems by simply getting recognition giving out of the closet and by making it *visible!*

Igniting a Recognition Revolution

You have to become a "recognition revolutionary" to make recognition visible. You must fight to get your company's recognition giving into the limelight.

Encourage managers to get out and walk around because it still rates high in the eyes of employees; get the process and guidelines for recognition giving well known through regular communications and education; make sure recognition which *is* being given is talked about and seen; and be a positive example of personally giving recognition.

Making recognition more visible will make it happen more often in the workplace. By increasing recognition visibility you will *see* improved performance and attitude results!

Go Get'em Giving Ideas

Follow these four ideas to increase visibility and make it a core principle behind your Real Recognition™ initiatives.

1: From the many employee interviews I have conducted for companies, they wish senior and middle managers would make themselves more visible. Employees want them to "see" what *they* are doing. Employees want to feel their contributions on the job and for the company are acknowledged and appreciated. If you want to catch people doing things right you have to make time to play catch! This action speaks volumes to your employees.

2: Company policies, processes, programs and guidelines need to be known by everyone. An organization I just worked with had a management driven program for giving movie pass certificates for exceptional staff performance. Once learned of, employees were curious if they could also nominate their colleagues. Whatever the guidelines are, make them known so everyone can help promote a recognition culture.

3: Create opportunities to celebrate and display recognition. Use newsletters, intranet websites, bulletin boards, etc., to share pictures, honors, customer acknowledgements, and awards. That way staff can spread the recognition around even longer. When projects are completed take time out for donuts or pizza, or whatever would fit the taste buds of your employees.

4: Leading by example is by everyone not just leaders by title. That's right. It's not just managers who are in leadership positions. Each employee needs to bear the weight of responsibility in giving recognition to peers, subordinates and their managers. Leadership is an action verb not just a position. Everyone owns recognition.

14.

STATE YOUR PREFERENCES

The more you know about people the better you can give the Real Recognition™ way.

I remember someone suggesting my electronic newsletter was too long in length. So I thought I had better ask my newsletter subscribers for their preferences rather than jump to any rash decisions. (For the benefit of readers you can subscribe to the Real Recognition E-Zine, an electronic monthly newsletter, by visiting our website at **www.RealRecognition.com**.)

Some of my recent clients are picking up on this concept and the key principle of "finding out first." Take the time to do either a formal survey of staff to identify preferences or by other informal methods such as focus groups.

Best of all is always creating a one-to-one opportunity. The return on investment (ROI) of time in observing, asking, and discovering what an employee likes, dislikes, aspires to and fears is *immense!* Incorporate this knowledge into improving what and how you will show appreciation and give praise to your employees.

Go Get'em Giving Ideas

Here are two things you can do to follow the principle of "know more to give more."

First, plan in time to spend at least 10 minutes with each of your employees and just ask, "How do you most like to be recognized or acknowledged for the contributions you make on the job?" Listen. Make notes.

Second, keep a written or permanent database record of what you find out. Then choose *one* way you could use this information to give *better* recognition to that individual, and then just DO IT! Repeat and rinse with others.

15.

ATTENTION ON RETENTION

Following a family vacation across the northern states and provinces of North America as well as speaking on a panel at an annual conference of association executives, I learned some more about the importance of paying attention to the retaining of employees. This principle can have a significant impact on the results of your recognition programs and practices.

The panel's topic was "Playing for Keeps – Improving Staff Retention." These non-profit organizations were looking for ways to compete with corporations to retain high performing staff. And I was being called upon for my expertise on employee recognition.

The message was clear from my panel colleagues that you have to know the job you're hiring for, recruit and hire right, even using objective behavioral testing, have a solid and a meaningful organizational culture, provide continuing education or opportunities, have both retention and reward and recognition strategies, and be willing to be coached in human resource and performance improvements.

How many organizations have retention strategies?

When I polled the attendees in the room as to how many of them had an active retention strategy, no more than 10 percent raised their hands. This was quite revealing.

So note the principle here. If you don't have a strategy and system in place to retain and recognize your employees, how do you expect to keep your staff? Today's workplace organizations will continue to lose and fail to attract the kind of employees to produce the results they need without a plan.

Which is the reason why I created the "3R's Audit" focusing on Results, Retention and Recognition to find out where the gaps are in an organization. You can request your own copy by e-mailing me at ***info@RealRecognition.com*** and putting "3R's Audit" in the subject heading.

Go Get'em Giving Ideas

In order to pay more attention to retention, try the following:

1. Check out and see if *your* organization has a written strategy for retaining employees and one for recognizing and rewarding them. If they don't, bring this up at your next management meeting to address this gap. Get acting on it if you do have one. Create one if you don't. Call me if you need help.

2. In the Chinook Health Region of Alberta, Canada, I learned they have created an "R Team" to address retention and recruitment issues. Make up your own team to recognize individuals and actively address issues that would help keep your employees for the longer term.

Everyone needs to "play for keeps."

16.

RECOGNIZING POTENTIAL

When a similar topic comes up twice in one week I like to grab onto it as a possible trend. The subject I am talking about is "potential."

In preparing to speak to members of an association comprised of municipal finance officers at their annual conference, I conducted numerous interviews with managers and employees to look at their retention and recognition strengths and issues.

I was impressed with one municipality which showed a strong commitment to valuing their people and the employee loyalty to the organization by hiring from within. They had caught the vision of Giving the Real Recognition Way.

Twist on Hiring Within

Nothing new you may say. But would you promote or move a loyal employee to a position they were not directly qualified for? There's the twist and a secret principle to grapple with and think about. Recognize potential and not just achievements.

Risky? Perhaps. But it certainly promotes growth potential for the employee.

If the employee wants to change jobs and is prepared to study and gain the necessary education for the new position, what better acknowledgment of an employee's current contribution and their future potential.

On a similar train of thought, Colleen Lundy, from Saskatchewan Government Insurance (SGI) Canada once wrote me saying, "Perhaps we pass over good candidates by repeatedly giving the special assignments and projects to the 'tried and tested.'"

You can end up overburdening those who always get the projects and advancement, and can risk losing them to burnout or being taken advantage of.

You can even risk losing those *not* given the opportunities to develop themselves because they feel slighted, overlooked, and want the chance to enhance their skills.

Colleen shared the following: "I believe that by recognizing someone's potential – and by allowing them to manage a task or create a new procedure or just plain something new – that this can speak a thousand words. To me, it is important to recognize potential, grant freedom, go with the flow, follow-up and provide support, encouragement and feedback along the way."

I think she's right! It's Giving the Real Recognition Way.

Go Get'em Giving Ideas

1. Know your employees' potential. Find out before formal performance reviews who is itching for a change OR what areas of interest they have beyond your department.

2. Make sure you share with other managers the names of staff that are looking for a change.

3. Make HR policies and procedures more flexible as far as job qualifications. We all need to learn to trust.

4. Talk to staff about projects. Ask if they would ever be interested in something new. You may be surprised!

17.

UNEXPECTED GIVING

One of several power principles for giving Real Recognition™ is the Principle of Expectation.

Everyone has a perceived level of expected recognition. When you exceed it or give the unexpected you increase the value of the recognition given. You create magic in an individual's life.

Let me illustrate.

In the city of London, Ontario where I once lived they hosted the Canada Summer Games and witnessed the rising young athletic stars of Canada.

A special and fun activity started spreading at these Canada Games. From athletes to volunteers, all were sharing lapel pins from their teams, province, or city, and proudly wore them on jackets and hats. It seems the trading of pins became the name of the "real games."

Pamela Waeland, then director of public relations at 3M Canada, was able to present the medals at one of the award ceremonies, as 3M was a major sponsor of the Games.

With approval of the organizers, and noting that the giving of the actual medals was of foremost importance, Pam was going to give something else.

Pam recalls presenting the silver medalist his shiny silver medal. She shook his hand. The medal and presentation was the *expected*.

After this, she then presented him with a shiny 3M-logo lapel pin. The medalist was ecstatic!! You would have thought he had won the gold medal instead. Here was the *unexpected*.

By being aware of the principle of what was expected, and then seeing what was currently important to a majority of people (like the lapel pin trading), the simple act of *adding* the unexpected created an even stronger memory association for this sports event.

Keep this principle in mind in your recognition practices by striving to vary the recognition you give by looking out for the degree of expectation.

And never underestimate the power of the unexpected!

Go Get'em Giving Ideas

1. Ask employees BEFORE the exit interview. Take time to ask employees while they are still with you, what kinds of recognition they like to receive. You'll be amazed how candid people will be.

2. Keep a database. Record staff and their interests, needs and wants with respect to work, personal and family balance, and types of recognition. This will be a tool to draw upon for ideas.

3. Be observant. Always be looking and listening for what people like. The example of the fad over lapel pins was observed and maximized to full advantage.

4. Always meet the level of recognition expectation. Someone who slaves over a project for weeks and receives no formal acknowledgement will think twice before taking on another

project. But the trickier and more rewarding task is to plan to exceed this level and shoot for the unexpected recognition.

18.

INDIVIDUAL VERSUS GROUP RECOGNITION

Many times when I ask managers for questions they may have regarding employee recognition, the issue of individual versus group recognition often comes up. A principled driven approach will allow you to give the Real Recognition™ way.

Some of the issues that can often stir up this question are:

1. Equity: Inequity of the level of effort or performance given by each team member.
2. Worth: Perception that it is wrong to even single people out and team recognition is the only way to go.
3. Philosophy: Concerns from situations like a unionized philosophy where recognition may be seen as being for everyone and not just one single person.

Let's examine each of these issues and see what recognition principles we can learn from them.

Equity

No matter where you and I go we will always find that human performance varies as much as people do.

The main reason for the concern comes when there are discrepancies in the performance of one or more individuals. People don't like to see everyone receive an award or acknowledgement for some achievement, when one or two people didn't perform well at all.

It's as bad as my schooldays when we *all* had to stay in after school because one student misbehaved.

For the most part this is a management issue of *not* dealing with poor performance. This can be easily done through setting expectations, listening, providing skills and resources, following up on actions taken, giving feedback and ongoing praise and of course, redirection. It also means dealing directly with negativity and identifying performance gaps right away.

In fact a good team should only be made up of competent players on the team. This should prevent a majority of the problems associated with team member "unworthiness" for recognition.

More often than not there will be the undisputed Most Valuable Player (MVP). So when it is clearly observed that one team player contributed significantly to the goal, recognize that individual.

Invite the star players on the team to assist in bringing others up the ladder. Think of Shaquille O'Neal from the Miami Heat pulling up teammate Dwyane Wade with him.

At the same time, acknowledge the rest of the team for their overall success. Be specific, include everyone's name, and tell each of them how they all made a difference. This principle often gets missed in the universal and global "well done."

Share the wealth and spread the stories of what your teams are collectively doing right. As just one example I checked out the website of the University Libraries of Notre Dame and discovered some great examples posted of the tales of their achievement and their group's recognition of one another.

Create a team fan club and acknowledge what they have collectively and individually contributed.

Worth

Is it wrong to single someone out? No it is not wrong. It is only incorrect if you put someone down in front of others.

Acknowledging them and expressing appreciation for their work is never wrong. Remember most of us desire receiving some form of recognition for our contributions. What is important is to respect individual wishes for private or public types of recognition.

The key principle here is to be constantly looking for every individual performance that warrants praise and to give it on an ongoing basis. Make time to get to know *all* team members.

Use newsletters or intranet websites to share team member snapshots indicating contributions to the team as a way of mixing individual and group recognition.

Philosophy

Do you remember the Gestalt psychology principle of "the sum of the whole is greater than the sum of its parts?"

Team or group recognition should always exceed that of the individual(s) who shine(s). Using a sports analogy, the team wins the cup or pennant and *then* they acknowledge the MVPs. The group is still greater than the individual. That attitude has to be top of mind.

It's important to have clear measurable performance indicators to show why someone truly contributed the most. So this can range from sales performance and other business results analogous to homeruns and goals. Measurable results help eliminate disputes over who really are the "star" players.

Bottom-line is remembering that it is always individuals who make up a team.

Go Get'em Giving Ideas

1. Create a clear and defined recognition philosophy. Beliefs are what propel behaviors. Write up what recognition is. Why are you giving it? Draft some guiding principles. Define the performance criteria.

2. When there is a requirement or expectation for group recognition, give both group and individual recognition. Focus on the group first and individuals second. Provide ongoing performance feedback to prevent non-performers and the perceived recognition inequity.

19.

CLAIMING THE HOLIDAY GOLDMINE

When the holiday season is getting started for some and just around the corner for others, you have the best opportunity in the world to discover recognition ideas.

Go digging for recognition principles. Be all ears and listen. Be all eyes and observe. Two ears and two eyes will be all the tools you really need. It will guarantee you being able to give the Real Recognition™ way.

Look & Listen

I have heard all kinds of people talk out loud about their Christmas or holiday season gift wish list. I have even heard descriptive accounts of what people *don't* like or want as well.

Watch as people receive office or workplace party or personal gifts and *look* how they react and *listen* to their comments. Make a mental note and until you can write or add this to your file on this person. All this keen detective work will help you create a bounty of recognition ideas for the current or following year.

Listen as people talk about what they are getting for others and then perhaps ask if they desire those same items as well. We tend to shop in familiar places which we personally like when we are shopping for others. You may tap into favorite stores and generate some ideas to store away.

Now, after the holidays listen with a slightly different focus.

We all love to share what we got from family and friends. Pay careful attention to non-verbal signs along with the verbal sharing of what people really *loved* from gifts received.

Typically, we just join in with the conversation. This time it's a chance to mine some gems for potential ideas for personal and meaningful recognition.

So make sure you tap this holiday goldmine!

Go Get'em Giving Ideas

1. Take time out to make notes on what you have heard already of people's gift wish list. If you haven't started one already make the time to create an employee profile to record your observations.

Make a note in your computer follow up system or planner, to listen up on your return to work *after* the holidays. The usual small talk from everyone on gifts received will be rich with ideas.

20.

WRITE WITHIN THE CARDS

In receiving Bill Cates' weekly e-zine or electronic newsletter (just visit his website at www.referralcoach.com), I read his comments about receiving holiday cards which were either unsigned or were just the preprinted signatures. His own observations and feedback from his clients were that such practices left a feeling of lack of sincerity and did little to build positive relationships.

His comments substantiate findings I gained from research in the insurance industry a few years ago. Consider these principles and apply them to your Real Recognition™ giving.

In speaking directly with clients of insurance representatives, I discovered they all wanted to hear more frequently from their representative. They acknowledged getting birthday cards and holiday cards, but they all commented on the apparent lack of concern they felt via the cards received because they *just* had the signature of the insurance representative and nothing else.

When asked what else they expected and what their insurance representative could do, the suggestions were things like:

- Add personal comments about the client's family
- Purely wishing the client well and indicating they would be in touch with them in the New Year
- Respectful humor
- Sharing a quick update from the representative's own life and/or family
- Including an article, bookmark or inspirational quotation card.

Anyone can sign his or her name in a card. The key is what *value* you can add to the card that builds relationships.

The same applies for any acknowledgement, thanks and congratulations you write to people.

Go Get'em Giving Ideas

1. With birthday cards for employees, friends, and customers, make time to write a short note inside that connects your relationship with that person. The card is just the medium. Your words are what people really want to see… and feel.

2. Be on the lookout for tangible items to include in cards you mail out. Whether it is an article or something small and thin, we all love to have something in addition to the card. Even a sticker!

21.

GOOD MORNING! GOOD MORNING!
TO YOU!

If you ever catch some of the great TV coverage of the Olympic Games, your local TV broadcaster may be using some of the very memorable commercials that always seem to accompany major sports events like this.

Maybe you remember the commercial from a few years ago. It was for the surprising product, Viagra, which capitalized on the well known and catchy tune of "Good Morning!" from the classic Broadway and Hollywood movie musical "Singing In The Rain" made famous by actors Debbie Reynolds, Gene Kelly and Donald O'Connor.

The song (and not the product being promoted, of course!) is a reminder of how important it is to make the time to say "good morning" to your peers and to the employees you work with in your organization.

This is no small thing. In fact it is an important start to Giving the Real Recognition Way.

My interviews with employees when I am preparing to provide training or consultation to managers reveals this one simple act is becoming increasingly rare. Not only do the managers walk right by them, they often do not even refer to the employee by name. Greet employees properly and use their name.

Those leaders and managers who made time to say hello and acknowledged employees by their first name were consistently rated as excellent examples of giving recognition towards all employees. A person's name is still music to their ears.

So when leaders ask me "Where should we start?" I strongly suggest looking at the first words out of their mouths each morning.

Go Get'em Giving Ideas

1. Do your own self-assessment this week. Start by tallying up the number of times *you* give a warm greeting to someone you see for the first time. When the person is known to you, add the person's first name following the greeting.

2. Now keep this going as a regular habit. The following week start noticing people's facial and non-verbal reactions as you greet them warmly. You will find a positive reaction to this simple behavior.

22.

MEETINGS THAT MATTER

I need you all to know that some of our electronic newsletter subscribers are doing absolutely incredible things with respect to giving employee recognition.

In doing my regular internet searching I stumbled across subscriber Fay Alexander's great work at the University of Alberta School of Business. Before Fay retired she used to be the general manager of about 50 support staff at the U of A Business School. Learn from the principles she applied in Giving the Real Recognition Way.

In a presentation of what she and her staff do to recognize each other I learned the value of consistency in not only holding but also improving upon regular staff meetings. How many staff meetings have you sat in where you were watching the clock? You won't do that at Fay's meetings!

Look at the following list to discover principles for making excellent meetings:

- Monthly, noon-hour meetings
- Fun, informative and interactive
- Bring bag lunch – juice/coffee and desserts provided
- Often have theme with decorated room and tables
- Door prizes!
- Staff set the agenda
- Dean or associate dean attends and reports
- Can have guest speakers on requested topics
- Some meetings are just for fun

Do you see some valuable principles you can follow? See if you agree with me on the following principles that I dug out of the above practices.

1. Consistency (have done this for four years!)
2. Valuable content (fun and learning)
3. Creating a memorable environment (décor)
4. Reward attendance (food and door prizes)
5. Ownership and involvement (staff input and ideas)
6. Senior management support (they report not dictate)
7. Fun (how come this is so difficult in some places?)

When you have great meetings like this, people *want* to be there. Fay notes that attendance has increased over the 4 years of holding meetings using these creative practices.

You can probably guess that "meetings" are far from all that Fay is doing right. Her team created a whole shopping list of wonderful ideas they are doing, including a unique idea of sharing "Aqua Babies" with one another. Fay is a real pro and a great example of "giving people Real Recognition™."

Fay received a copy of my booklet "101 Ways to Give EVERYDAY Real Recognition" for her example and for sharing of her employee recognition successes. You can find articles and other helpful resources at our website at www.RealRecognition.com. And you can order your own copy of the "101 Ways to Give EVERYDAY Real Recognition" booklet to stimulate your thinking.

Go Get'em Giving Ideas

1. Take some ordinary experience from work, like a staff meeting, and then go through the principles identified above and ask: "How could I make this workplace experience a

positive expression in acknowledging the worth of the people who work here?"

2. Now you can't do this all on your own. Get a group of staff together that is equally committed to appreciating others worth and potential. Make this your recognition team for whatever work experience you have chosen to enhance or change. Now go and make it happen!!

23.

WHO HAS MADE A DIFFERENCE
IN YOUR LIFE?

Who in your past has had the most significant influence on your life to make you the kind of person you are today?

Now here is the point I want to make.

Have you ever told them of the difference they made to you and have you thanked them. This will be the most important Giving the Real Recognition Way you will ever make.

A few years ago my "Aunt" Cath died in England at the age of 86 peacefully in her sleep.

Her contribution and influence in my life was raising me for the first two years of my life after my mother died giving birth to me. My Dad would pick me up after work and look after me most evenings until he remarried when I was two.

As I read my Aunt Cath's letters over the years and saw how positive she always was, I realized that a lot of those same qualities must have rubbed off on me during those critical developmental years.

And how grateful I am that a few years ago I made the time to write her and tell her how much I appreciated all that she had done for me.

Her passing is all the more peaceful knowing I thanked her for the greatest gift she could give me...

...a Mother's love.

Go Get'em Giving Ideas

1. Before it gets too late in years or with the unexpected happenings of life, make a goal this week to express your thanks verbally or in writing to a significant person who has made a difference in your life. Take care and time in the writing, just don't delay in the sending.

2. Send someone flowers while they are alive, and while they can still enjoy them. Don't wait until their funeral. This was my personal regret.

24.

DON'T FORGET THE HOME FRONT

One of the reasons I started focusing on employee recognition was because of not receiving much recognition in my personal life as a child and teenager.

So without that example from my home, and that's without any disrespect to my parents who also lacked the same in their own childhood, I have to continually learn to do a much better job in my own life and at home.

And hence the maxim that it is often the teacher who needs to learn the most.

So while I focus much of the recognition giving in this book and in my consulting to be in the workplace, I would be a fool to say to you, "Turn off the recognition switch when you leave the plant, field or office." Make sure you transfer this principle into your daily life.

In fact, if you are not actively giving recognition to your spouse, partner, children and family members, you will have more problems than you can handle. And it will also affect your personal performance on the job. If you're not showing appreciation where it means the most, at home, you will be a lousy giver of recognition at work.

Getting Into The Giving Mindset At Home

You have to acquire a recognition giving mindset no matter where you are. It's developing the attitude of Giving the Real Recognition Way both day and night.

While I was in the office supply store Staples this week, in the month of March, I saw some of those die-cut Post-It® Notes that 3M produces on sale. Now while most people were checking out the balloon shapes, the flowers, and shamrocks, yours truly dug really deep and found a lonely pack of heart shaped notes left over from Valentines Day.

You can probably see where I am going.

It was fun writing some pun play on words, and cute lines (those who know me well will attest to my pun-ny sense of humor) on these heart notes, and then placing them in different places for my wife to eventually find them, like: "You drive me crazy" placed on the steering wheel of our car.

Now my wife is wondering after finding a few where the next one is going to appear. Whew! The expectations are high. But the constant smile on her face as she finds another note is priceless and well worth it.

Go Get'em Giving Ideas

1. While recognition is often talked about as a workplace phenomenon, remember we all crave to be appreciated both young and old and especially in the home. If you are not regularly giving your family members recognition would you please start? They need it desperately, and besides, it's fun!!

2. So the last point was a call to action. Now plan what you are going to do to say or show your appreciation and praise for your spouse, partner or children by the end of today.

Let me know of some of the experiences you had doing this. E-mail me a short account of what you did and how it was received and we'll consider using your submission and create a book on "Real Recognition™ on the Home Front." Simply send your story, example, or short idea in an e-mail to me with "Home Front" in the subject heading directly to my attention to: RoySaunderson@RealRecognition.com.

25.

WORKING WITH DIFFICULT PEOPLE

When I was speaking at a conference for municipal administrators several of the audience members there were challenged with dealing with negative, nagging, difficult people in the workplace. Never a nice or an easy thing to deal with. I was most surprised at the stunning frequency of the problem within, in particular, municipal government.

Then I reviewed a book summary entitled "How to Work with Just About Anyone: A Three-step Solution for Getting Difficult People to Change," by Lucy Gill (Published by Fireside/ Simon and Schuster 1999 ISBN 0-684-85527-5, 206 pages).

Negativity will destroy any attempts at giving recognition. You have to eliminate negative behaviors to make recognition effective and a part of Giving the Real Recognition Way.

Gill's book does a great job of giving some practical tips. So this is particularly for my new friends of municipal clerks and treasurers whom I spoke to. If you don't get rid of the negatives at work it will sap you dry along with the positive energy of recognition giving right out of the window.

Dealing with negative behavior, whether at work or at home, can be solved with these three steps according to Gill:

1. Try to get to the heart of the matter in finding a solution.
2. Determine what problem-solving methods you should avoid so you don't perpetuate the conflict and create more problems.
3. Choose a different and even surprising approach to solve the problem and keep it solved.

In managing the prevention and management of nonproductive behaviors Gill suggests you consider how difficult behavior is often reinforced. You'll usually find that people use the same solution which of course never brings new results. This is usually described as the definition for insanity!

The solution then is to try something completely different. Use a completely new approach and then choose your response very carefully.

So why do we keep getting caught up in the same negative behaviors?

1. We get caught up in the web of our very own logic mindset.
2. We don't realize we are doing the same things over and over again.
3. We can't think of anything better to try.

These are just a few great points from this book on a critical subject that can poison any good you strive to do in giving people recognition in the workplace.

Go Get'em Giving Ideas

1. OK. You've read some of the points above. Now chose just *one* thing you are going to do differently today in dealing with that negative person at work. Write it down in your planner, on your "to do" list, Outlook® or whatever personal electronic system you are using. Stamp out the negatives!

2. After trying the above idea out now do a self-critique on yourself. Write down how you did and what would you do differently next time, along with what you learned from using this tactic? Learn from your own doing.

26.

PRINCIPLE OF EXPECTATION

Giving the Real Recognition Way is a method based upon solid principles of human behavior. In looking at how employee recognition is typically carried out in organizations I have learned that it is rarely principle driven but rather program driven.

Take a look at the Principle of Expectation.

Each person has a perceived level of expected recognition. For some it may be minimal while for others it may be quite large. When you exceed this expected level of recognition or give the unexpected you automatically increase the value of the recognition given.

The key then is to know what each employee expects for the different types of recognition, the frequency of occurrence, and for what acts is acknowledgement expected.

With the upfront investment of time in finding out what employees want, the anticipated quantity and frequency, you are prepared to truly give Real Recognition™.

Too many times employees leave an organization because they did not feel appreciated for the contributions they made on the job. This is a needless loss and one which can be easily prevented by understanding the Principle of Expectations and other recognition principles.

You can see why a cookie cutter approach to recognition giving does not work. We all have different expectations. Do you know what kind of recognition your employees expect from you?

Go Get'em Giving Ideas

1. Determine to find out what expectations your employees have of you for the recognition they are looking for. Ask where there satisfaction level is on a 10-point scale in meeting their recognition expectations. Question them on one thing you could personally do which could move you closer to a 10.

2. Do some personal introspection on the kind of recognition you expect from others. Most leaders require much less recognition than their direct reports. Examine the types of contributions you make and your preferences for the type of recognition you like. Start to better understand that there are differences between people. Now pair up with a colleague or spouse/partner and talk about their expectations. Share your own expectations with them.

Section 2

35 Tips for Employers and Managers on Giving the Real Recognition Way

27.

EVERYDAY UNSUNG HEROES

This week my wife made me aware of the many everyday unsung heroes that I personally take for granted. So I have to be up front and state that this tip is brought to you by my good wife who I often learn a great deal from on the topic of Giving the Real Recognition Way.

In the city where I live in, we have a weekly recycling pick up as well as our regular garbage pick up.

We were cleaning up in our house and so we put out an unusually large number of plastic bottles in our recycling.

So early in the morning when the sound of the recycling truck was heard, my wife was hoping this increase of materials would not be a problem. She hovered by the front door for the driver's approach to our property.

As he was dumping the sorted, paper, glass and plastics, my wife went outside and thanked him for dealing with the large amount of recycling garbage.

He smiled and simply said, "It was neatly organized. No problem."

Now I don't know about you, but I have never thanked my garbage collector before. I wondered how often a member of the public had ever thanked this man.

Go Get'em Giving Ideas

1. Think of all the behind-the-scenes people who make your life easier and better. Write up a list of at least five people who

make your world a better place but you rarely see them. Make the time this week to send a letter or card expressing your appreciation to them and/or their boss for what they do and how you benefit.

2. How about your family members? I realized that I verbally thank my children but I have *never* sent a written thank you. I followed all the principles of being specific and stating how I had benefited and sent each of my children at home separate cards for major chores going on right now at the end of summer. Even family members deserve some variety in appreciation.

28.

FROM PRESENTATION TO CELEBRATION

I personally enjoy my work so much because I get to talk to employees and managers about recognition, good and bad, and what keeps them staying with their organizations.

Last week, I spoke with a public sector awards recipient who had developed a new method that improved quality and saved time and money. He was nominated and received awards from his own federal department and from the federal government as a whole.

In comparing the two awards and accompanying events, he indicated how he considered his own department's as a "celebration" while the government event he described simply as a "presentation." The tip for you to apply in making the Real Recognition™ way happen is turn your presentations into star-studded celebrations.

You can probably envision the differences. Let me list just a few items that stood out for this individual.

A Celebration

For this award recipient a "Celebration" meant:

- The set up of the event created a warm and positive atmosphere. So make a note of the environment and ask if it generates a celebratory picture.
- Quick tour of headquarters where recipients were greeted and acknowledged even before the awards event began later that day.
- Whole day event with fellow recipients getting to know one another and share ideas. If it is ideas we are

celebrating then we need to share and cross-pollinate with other ideas.

- Display of previous recipients and their accomplishments in storyboard fashion which helped create ongoing pride and a sense of legacy in the past.
- "Top brass" were there for the whole time with a full dinner.
- A senior leader sat at each table along with the recipients which helped instill a sense of connection and breakdown barriers.
- Great amount of time to mingle and connect which allowed for the building of positive relationships.
- Spouses/partners were flown in for the event at no personal expense which just made the whole experience more personal and a true celebration that could be shared with loved ones.
- Plaque/certificate had on it specific wording of what the person did to merit the award, rather than a generic nonspecific statement.

A Presentation

In contrast, let's look at what the word "Presentation" conjured up and actually was to this person:

- 5 o'clock after work affair for everyone which had this rushed feeling or sense of "let's get this over with."
- Quick, sterile rehearsal, that lost all real meaning other than task driven.
- Canned speech by senior leaders with nothing specific to individuals and their accomplishments.
- The on stage "Grip & Grin" of folks filing on, fast handshake, smile and leave. Plain and simply, it was impersonal.

- Just department people present with no family members, which was probably just as well considering the way it was done.
- Plaque had a short generic statement of award name and no specifics.

You get the picture... and most importantly, the feeling. Which approach took the Real Recognition™ route?

Go Get'em Giving Ideas

1. Get some paper and create two columns. Head one column with "celebration" and the other with "presentation." Add more ideas to the ones I listed above. Which column would you rather have? Remember awards "honor experiences."

2. The Go Get'em Giving Idea above was fun and probably easy to do. Now I want you to answer what your organization is doing. Are you creating celebrations or presentations? With list in hand go and enlist the right people, influence the right people, infiltrate the right people... whatever it takes to make your next awards event an experience and *not* another boring awards meeting. Go celebrate!

29.

KEEPING THINGS TOP OF MIND

One of the important things to be done to keep recognition giving alive and well is to be constantly communicating and promoting it. You have to always make recognition giving top of mind which is a hard but necessary tip to apply.

There are three basic categories that communication actions fall under, namely:

1. Face-to-face communication
2. Written or printed communication, and
3. Electronic communication

A wonderful idea that fits the "written communication" category came from a meeting I once had with a Canadian federal human resources manager from the Department of National Defense.

Here is what Annette Reichert, former Team Leader for Awards and Recognition, and her team did.

They produced those erasable whiteboards with the departmental and awards name identifiers and the website URL imprinted on them. After these graphics and wording came the traditional "To Do" list title and underneath came the typical 10 spaces and a check off box for each item on the far right. However, the first item on the "To Do" list was already written in *and* checked off. In English and French it reads "Thank someone today."

Annette concludes, "It really works for us. The white boards are a hot item, and a good reminder to all who receive them to thank someone everyday."

Great idea, Annette!

The principle this communicates is "people come first, tasks come second" by putting recognition at the top of the list. Second, as an important tip it is creating a physical reminder with endorsement and financial commitment from senior leaders. Thirdly, it is a creative, novel and fun way to get people's attention.

Make sure you provide the erasable kind of markers!

Go Get'em Giving Ideas

1. Take on just *one* of the communication categories to play around with. Brainstorm simple and doable ideas that can be implemented within the next 30 days. One group from a recent workshop is going to utilize existing large whiteboards they have and make sure there is a different positive message about employee recognition on it *everyday*. This is a very simple method and one with little or no cost attached.

2. For the more adventurous and those with perhaps more funding available, try a three-pronged approach. Use all three of the categories and come up with one realistic, manageable idea for *each* category. Using the different mediums will help reinforce the message with variety. Variety is the spice of life and guaranteed to warm up your recognition initiatives.

30.

IF SCHOOL BUS DRIVERS CAN DO IT

Here's an observation from the streets where I live and a simple tip you can put into practice.

In November and spurred on by the Dutch traditions of those celebrating St. Nicholas in the beginning of December, smart retailers start selling those large chocolate initial letters. Often they can be bought on sale for a dollar or cheaper. Good chocolate too!

My wife overheard a school bus driver who has about 30 children on his bus, buying a matching chocolate letter for the first name of each of the students on his bus. Thirty dollars and he will probably have the best-behaved kids of all the bus drivers in the city.

Now one can imagine that this type of action is not new to this bus driver. School bus drivers don't get paid a lot of money. Unlike the comic-strip character, Crankshaft, you mostly have to love children to drive a bus full of them.

So this bus driver is fueled by caring and has taken the time to make sure he has the chocolate letter representing the first letter of each child's name. A relatively small investment of money but it comes at a sacrifice for a low-income earner.

Wouldn't you love to be a bug on a backpack the day he gives his chocolate letters out?

Go Get'em Giving Ideas

1. This kind of idea works best for departments or companies of a small manageable size. Why not replicate it and buy some

chocolate letters for your employees? If a Wal-Mart runs out, find a local Dutch store in your neighborhood.

2. I love to read, and I am a devoted fan of the late Og Mandino, an inspirational writer. At one holiday work party I gave each of my employees a different copy of one of his books along with a bookmark with a special quote on it tailored to each respective person. So why not allow what you love to come through with what you give.

31.

WHERE SELDOM IS HEARD...

In that old Western cowboy song, "Home on the Range," the chorus goes on to say "where seldom is heard a discouraging word...."

Catch the recognition tip you can try out in the following account. One conference session attendee where I was speaking asked me what they could do to encourage managers to give employees recognition. The vague connection here is that I immediately thought of "where seldom is heard an *encouraging* word..." and then quickly jumped to employee recognition.

Therein lies the key to the solution... an "encouraging" word.

"Encourage" means "to give heart."

Managers have to give from the heart to be really leaders and *not* just managers. They must learn to care about people and then demonstrate that caring and concern.

The other essential is managers have to hear regular *words* about employee recognition. Most important is hearing words of example from senior leaders. This must then be relayed as an expectation through management forums, leadership development sessions, and performance and accountability measures.

Another successful strategy is to share the stories of success of employee recognition giving. Now that is really perpetuating encouraging words.

Too often I hear about the stories of wonderful recognition initiatives, and examples of managers who truly honor their employees…and then I ask, "So has this story been written up, put on the web, in a newsletter, told by the CEO?" And the answer is more often than not, "no!"

So take advantage of this lost opportunity and publicize the need for the "encouraging word."

Go Get'em Giving Ideas

1. Survey your managers on how they best like to receive communication… the *word*. Learn from this because the sources given will help you to know where to focus but not to eliminate the lesser-frequented ideas. A bulletin board near the cafeteria may just capture the attention of one person tired of accessing the intranet.

2. Remember there is a priority influence factor for the type of communication. Face-to-face is always valued greater than say technology. That's why Jack Welch of GE spent nearly half of his time out in the trenches talking with managers and employees. That kind of commitment truly created the "encouraging word."

32.

A NEW YEAR'S
RECOGNITION RESOLUTION

It's always pleasing for me to hear from some of my clients or even newsletter subscribers that they have created some strategic plans to implement recognition actions in their organization.

Perhaps many of you are also working on ways to improve how you will be improving your recognition initiatives.

Your goal for each New Year is to do whatever is necessary to make recognition giving increase in frequency and be felt more by employees.

Here's a simple tip for you. Simply compare where you are now with where you want to be.

ONE: Perhaps with formal recognition you know your awards ceremonies are too stiff and impersonal. You would like them to be warm, personal and true celebrations.

TWO: On an informal level you realize that departments are inconsistent with use of discretionary funds for recognizing project successes. While allowing flexibility you know there should be a greater degree of consistency than there is.

THREE: For the everyday recognition you have observed some managers are not giving any verbal feedback to their employees and their employees are letting you know. You obviously want more of these managers to be giving verbal praise and acknowledgement to their employees.

So now you have three scenarios of *current results* and *desired results*. As you compare one with each other you can probably see some *required changes* that can be made.

Itemize and prioritize the list of proposed changes and enlist appropriate individuals to champion and facilitate with others to make the changes actually happen.

Go Get'em Giving Ideas

1. Do an assessment of your current recognition practices. The further afield your employees are you may have to do a survey. Otherwise create focus groups or ask in staff meetings for employee and manager input.

2. Remember, if you are going to ask people for their perspective on employee recognition you had better guarantee you are going to act upon suggestions. There is nothing worse than getting people excited about change and then doing nothing. Especially about employee recognition.

33.

NOT BETTER LATE THAN NEVER

We've all heard the expression "better late than never."

Well in recognition giving that phrase just doesn't cut it. So become a master of this tip for being on top of Giving the Real Recognition Way.

In a recent public sector survey we conducted ninety-four percent (94%) rated "timely delivery of awards" as the highest in importance from a list of recognition program elements.

The longer the gap in time from the performance or achievement being acknowledged and the receipt of recognition or award, then the *intrinsic* value of the actual recognition diminishes.

Simply stated, the sooner the warranted recognition is given the shinier the star!

Example: Someone reaches an anniversary milestone and merits receiving a 5-year pin. However, the annual awards' meeting does not occur for yet another 11-months after the special day itself.

Instead of delaying such a process, have the managers or supervisors give pins on, or as close as possible within 48 hours of the anniversary date in the local department.

Then at the annual larger meeting or with the organization-wide celebratory event they can join others who started with the organization at the same time and perhaps receive a certificate along with the customary refreshments and honoring activities.

For those of you who are married use your wedding anniversary as a guide. You would *never* forget the day of your anniversary and you would always give a well worded card, a gift and possibly flowers, no matter what or when you might formally celebrate the anniversary with a dinner or trip.

Go Get'em Giving Ideas

1. What informal recognition can be given immediately to someone who is being acknowledged for a formal award achievement? Ensure formal award nominees get a letter within 24 to 48 hours of nomination receipt congratulating them on their nomination. Also thank the nominator for making the time to complete the process, thus encouraging people to submit nominations.

2. For everyday recognition take the time at the end of the day to reflect on just one or two people you can write a thank you card to or send out an e-mail. Remember to be specific and sincere in your wording.

34.

MAKING IT EASY TO GIVE

For some reason people tend to make giving employee recognition *too* hard to do.

Following my workshop sessions I insist on a 30-day homework assignment to implement a new skill or principle learned. The feedback from participants after the homework always includes how easy it was to do, with almost a sense of surprise and satisfaction in that observation.

Here are four easy tips to make recognition giving easier for you to put into practice.

1. Realistic Expectations

I acknowledge that workloads and demands are high. I always tell people to set goals that are realistic and doable. Better to do something once a week to start with, rather than setting yourself up for failure if tackling a daily task is unrealistic.

2. Personal Choice and Responsibility

Starting a new recognition giving behavior need not be an organizational goal. Better to get personal buy-in yourself by doing what you feel most comfortable with. I saw one case last month where one person did not agree with a team goal. Guess what? It didn't happen.

3. Ample Resources

Another key is to have tools, helpful techniques on hand, even a supply of cards, stickers, books, etc., to stimulate thinking and be an instant resource to draw upon when the time is right to give recognition.

Many organizations are creating "tool-kits," boxes with oodles of paper and materials including supplies such as thank you cards, congratulation cards, certificates, stickers, pamphlets, booklets and reminder cards to both cue oneself and items to send to others.

4. Accountability is Key

No follow up, no moving up. Progress is achieved when personal accountability is given for simple goals to make recognition happen. The easier the goal is the greater the guarantee of it actually happening. There is also a greater chance for ongoing change that means recognition can become a habit. Write it down, commit to someone else, and plan a date to follow-up on the goal.

Go Get'em Giving Ideas

1. Have peer-manager follow up on goals to see how you are doing with recognition giving. Literally set a one-month goal and agree to connect with a buddy or small group of fellow managers. While Giving the Real Recognition Way really is easy, if you don't hold yourself accountable to new behaviors nothing will ever change.

2. Start quarterly management forums. This need not be with an outside facilitator. Simply come together as a management team or peers and share your own best practices and solicit ideas for dealing with issues and concerns. Giving effective recognition can be a regular part of the agenda along with other human resources and organizational development topics.

35.

TARGETING YOUR EMPLOYEES

Giving the Real Recognition Way is most effective when it becomes part of how you approach everyday.

One way to get to this level is to target employees you will give recognition to.

For example, you may be finding it easier to give recognition just to people you like which only breeds favoritism in the eyes of those not receiving recognition and those who are cynical to recognition. So who are you going to target?

The key is to remember this tip:

All recognition giving is relationship building.

There are usually three groups of people we work with, i.e. peers, subordinates, and managers.

Top Down Recognition

Tradition has created the expectation that managers recognize employees. This type of recognition is still the most valued. How are you doing here? Who is someone you may have neglected? Reflect on their achievements and give some acknowledgement. Make a list of all the people you have been putting off praising.

Lateral Recognition

Next in value is recognition from peers. We can tend to take them for granted. Stop and reflect where you and your work would be if not for your colleagues? Who is contributing to your results? You may find quite a few people. Just take one at a time, even one a week if you have to.

Take time to send them a note or even an e-mail. Make sure you tell them specifically how they are making a difference to you personally.

Bottom Up Recognition

The least amount of recognition given is not to employees below but to mangers and senior leaders above us. It can be a lonely world at the top.

In my training sessions, most managers acknowledge in some of our practice exercises that this role is the most awkward for fear of how those above will perceive our actions.

Again, the practice of being very specific about what you are acknowledging negates the phony, sucking up kind of inferences that can be associated with recognizing a boss or person with senior leadership responsibilities.

Go Get'em Giving Ideas

1. Convergent Targeting. Another targeting method is to look for those people who do similar work as you do. Perhaps those who are contributors of a customer project you do not directly see too often are folks you haven't thanked recently.

2. Divergent Targeting. There are those completely removed from our direct roles but who contribute to the organization as a whole. I always take time to thank gardeners, janitors, and security personnel in companies I visit. You'll be amazed at the difference you can make.

36.

PRACTICE MAKES PERFECT??

One of the benefits of working with managers on giving effective recognition to employees is that I often get asked challenging questions.

A question repeated a couple of times over the last few sessions have been around the issue of practicing and monitoring your behavior in giving recognition. For example, I often draw upon Dr. Terry Paulson's powerful tip of carrying five pennies in one pocket and with the goal of giving five praises or compliments during the day. As you successfully achieve this you move one penny from one pocket to another and tally your results at the end of the day. I give other ideas as well.

This was challenged as being insincere and phony.

What do you think?

Becoming A Natural

Remember a large majority of managers are not naturals at giving recognition. In changing any performance I will not disagree that at first this *may* come across as insincere. You can often eliminate this by being very specific with the wording you choose to say and with the type of recognition you are giving. I would hope this would wipe out any observation of the mechanics of practicing.

Perfect Practice

So what is a person to do to bridge this sincerity gap?

Those of you who are sports inclined have often heard the term "practice makes perfect." Actually, this is not a true statement at all.

It is *perfect* practice that makes perfect. You have to do it right and then keep practicing doing it right. I constantly have to put reminder cues and systems in place to help keep me on track for giving credit where credit is due, along with expressions of thanks and appreciation. There is nothing wrong with that in my opinion. And so far, those receiving my recognition still seem to appreciate it, which is the bottom line.

Go Get'em Giving Ideas

1. What steps or systems do you need to put in place to become personally more consistent with giving recognition? Often a simple reminder in Outlook® or equivalent reminder system, your planner, and contact management system is all you really need to start practicing the fine art and skill of giving people Real Recognition™.

2. For actual face-to-face kinds of recognition there is no harm in scheduling in your day or week when you will do walkabouts and make contact with people. You can be observing and make direct verbal feedback and appreciative comments. Or you can go back and write down notes on what performance you saw that merits recognition. You may have heard some things you need to follow up on later. And observing and listening will help you discover what to give or say and how people like to be recognized.

37.

GIVING BETTER GROUP RECOGNITION

Several of my newsletter subscribers have wondered how to effectively recognize both the group's team efforts, as well as recognizing any special or extra contribution of one or more specific members of the group. Should that be done publicly as well, or as an additional recognition to the specific person aside from the group's recognition?

There is no "one way" in Giving the Real Recognition Way. But there are principles to follow that are always the same. For example, one tip to follow is to look at what you know about your group or team members first and then what you can do personally.

So let's say a team completes a project and you take them out for lunch or you plan a pizza/pot luck get together at work to recognize their achievement.

Staging the Celebration

One idea: personally acknowledge the group effort and mention the specific elements you know that each individual contributed to the project. Each person is mentioned and not left out.

Another idea: definitely acknowledge verbally the whole team. Ask each team member ahead of the celebration for input on who worked "above and beyond" on this project and have team members nominate the person who gets special recognition. This takes the focus off of you and any managerial bias. It allows for peer recognition.

Group recognition should always be public as a team and sometimes in front of other employees. Individual recognition may be given publicly or one-on-one. Don't forget to respect each person and find out their preferences for recognition.

Go Get'em Giving Ideas

1. Know your team. What is going to work best for your team, public or private? Make time to ask team members individually what they prefer. And ask as a group what they would like to do as teams to celebrate within the time and monetary constraints you have.

2. Know yourself. One of the harsh realities is the workloads and time pressures on making time to give recognition. What can you realistically do, and afford to do, to acknowledge group performance? Even a special group thank you card with specific comments sent to the whole team with a box or container of goodies to enjoy can mean the world.

38.

"AW! IT WAS NOTHING."

When you get going on effectively Giving the Real Recognition Way to all levels of employees, you start to realize people are not accustomed to receiving recognition as a positive experience in their lives.

Many of them give a comeback line after receiving a praise or compliment with something like, "Aw! It was nothing," or "It was just my job," or something along those words. In reality, they are negating the acknowledgment being given to them for various possible reasons – based on upbringing, societal learning, or just plain habit.

In our training programs we deal with why this happens and provide strategies on how to handle it personally, in order to prevent us from negating positive feedback given to us.

But what about those we give feedback or praise to who have not been on training programs and who still deflect the praise?

Teach them what you know. Give them the reason behind the "why" not to deflect positive praise and acknowledgement.

Teach them what you have experienced or learned that it is important to just accept such comments. Tell them to try their best to hold their tongue after receiving some positive commendation.

Teach them these four basic points:

1. Tell them first off to just say "thank you" after receiving a compliment. Then teach them they have to learn to just zip the lips after saying "thank you!"

2. Encourage them to simply smile at the person praising you. Bask in the warmth that the other person is sending your way. Accept the praising. It really is good!

3. Make eye contact where it is culturally appropriate. Often we look down, embarrassed when we hear good things about us. So look up, feel good and look the giver in the eyes. This is appropriate to most people from North American and European backgrounds but may not be the case for Asian and native Americans.

4. Use the person's name within your acknowledgment of the praise. Once you are accustomed to doing these actions and you get your confidence going you can say more than just, "thank you." Use their name and express appreciation to them personally for making the time to say something to you.

Go Get'em Giving Ideas

1. First point is how are *you* doing? Keep a tally or try to observe what you normally say after receiving praise and appreciation. Work on catching yourself and correcting any negative comments you may be making. You may be very surprised at how you are doing.

2. To help employees around you grow in accepting positive comments about themselves, find the right time to teach them. Share your own struggles in overcoming negative comments as an example. Tell them what you have learned to say and give examples. Encourage them to accept and bask in the glory of sincere appreciation.

39.

SHARING YOUR SUCCESSES

Some acts of recognition are not so much *us* having to think, say or do something.

Pay attention to this simple tip for making the Real Recognition™ way a bigger part of your organization. Often it can simply be a matter of orchestrating opportunities for others to give people recognition, and creating the right environment. Thus acknowledgement can come from others and does not always need to be from us.

In one consultation interview I learned again of the power of permitting employee recognition success stories to be shared in staff meetings.

The following simple actions added to any meeting agenda allows people to do at least something to making employee recognition top of mind:

- Share actions or examples of service principles or values which are followed within the organization.
- Practice in getting comfortable with blowing one's own horn by having meeting attendees stating recent accomplishments in one's personal or professional life.
- Role modeling of one another's successful work experiences so that others can have similar successes.
- Build awareness in managers and peers of the kinds of behaviors and achievements they should be recognizing.

Sandra Myers, an IBM sales manager was quoted in the 2003 summer issue of Sales and Marketing Management, that she used their weekly teleconference calls for her sales force to highlight a winning sales tactic.

Not only was this a chance to educate peers it also created a linkage for future mentoring by successful representatives for those who wanted more insights.

So make time to share and show you care.

Go Get'em Giving Ideas

1. Put success sharing on your meeting agendas. You can either open this spontaneously during the meeting or request people submit their names for consideration. You could role model an example of doing this when you first try it out.

2. Initially, you may have to coach people along or reinforce what a person thought was no big deal that it really is worthwhile for others to learn about. The key is to facilitate the process.

40.

WHY DO PEOPLE KEEP
THANK YOU CARDS?

During my training sessions I often ask the question, "Why do people keep thank you cards?"

To answer this question more scientifically I polled my Real Recognition E-zine subscribers (you can subscribe at www.RealRecognition.com) to get more specific input to from a quantitative perspective. The results below will provide you with sound tips to use when sending written praise or acknowledgements.

Here is what I asked my subscribers: "Please indicate the *most* important reason for why you personally re-read certain Thank You cards over others."

Research says...

Examine carefully what respondents were saying in the answers they gave and pull out the significance for what you should be doing to get people to re-read your Thank You cards:

- 59 percent want to recall the feelings of being acknowledged
- 26 percent want to recall the relationship between themselves and the sender
- 9 percent want to recall the action being acknowledged, and
- 6 percent want to recall the level of performance given

This again emphasizes the strong "feeling" component within the recognition experience.

Let's look at factors that people said were *very* important in keeping their thank you cards. I'll list them in the rank order for you. Again, take special note of these points and ask yourself what you can learn from these answers.

1. Sender writes the card versus assistant (84%)
2. Handwritten note is still better than typed (67%)
3. Specific wording in the acknowledgement (58%)
4. Relationship of the sender to you (52%)
5. Timeliness of card sent after the action (48%)
6. Ease of reading handwriting (40%)
7. Nature of task/action being acknowledged (37%)
8. Sender's choice of card (28%)
9. Mailed to home versus through office mail (5%)

Go Get'em Giving Ideas

1. The first four items above are your written Thank You card guidelines. Write the card yourself and make that handwritten, be specific with your wording on what is being recognized, and continuously develop a positive working relationship with your employees and peers.

2. How many of your thank you cards are being kept and re-read? While I don't want you to go out and do a survey on that question, just remember these important factors and you'll start getting more cards being kept by recipients than you ever had before.

41.

PRESERVING THE HEART

Each fall my wife and I usually put up preserves of a variety of bought or homegrown fruits and vegetables. The experience of doing this always brings back memories and allows us to enjoy the fruits of our labors in the cold winter season.

When the next holiday season comes along and as many faiths and customs give and receive gifts, why don't you ask yourself this question as you consider what to give to those around you at work or at home, "How can I preserve the *heart* of this individual?"

What do I mean when I say the "heart" of an individual?

I am talking about:

- warmth of relationships
- what that person stands for
- who they really are
- all the positive qualities they bring
- the essence of that person

And how do you do this? The answer to this question produces a powerful tip for making Giving the Real Recognition Way even more meaningful.

The answer to this question is to simply ask questions. Find out what people want to be, to have and to do. This is an all year round activity and one that should be pursued ever after. Learn about them and their interests. Discover what they love.

I recently found out that one person I was planning to give a gift to *really* loved chocolates. I found this out from this person's assistant. Sometimes this "heart preserving" takes a little extra effort, some patience over time and even a degree of inquisitive detective work.

So the decision was finally made to give this person expensive boxed and gift-wrapped chocolates with the store seal on the wrapping. The reward was seeing this person's eyes light up as they saw the store seal-label on the box and *knew* what was inside! This adult individual even started jumping up and down like a little kid. Imagine!

The automatic reaction was not only to hear the words, "Thank You!" but to also receive an enthusiastic hug.

I think you capture the picture.

So make time to preserve some hearts at work as well as at home during the next holiday season.

Go Get'em Giving Ideas

1. Preserving is the art of bottling things up that you like to enjoy later. Take time to capture memories by capturing photographs and video shots at work and share these pictures in newsletters, intranet or bulletin boards.

2. Don't worry if you are not ready this year. Make a plan to find out details of peoples likes, wants and interests so you know what it takes to preserve fellow worker's and employees hearts all year long.

42.

FROM A DISTANCE

As telecommuting increases and managers and supervisors become responsible for more distant field offices and virtual positions, the challenge of being able to give meaningful recognition increases.

I can't help thinking of the Bette Midler song that implies we are being watched "from a distance."

In a similar manner you have to watch from a distance by just increasing the use of other people's eyes, ears and mouths to know what your folks in the field are doing when you can't possibly be right there.

Who can you enlist assistance from?

- Actively solicit customer/client satisfaction surveys and comment directly to employees. Comment on letters and calls received about them.

- Actively ask supervisory staff to be truly "good watchers" and share with you just the good things going on. They can manage the problems and course corrections; you must be a major positive support.

- Have peers create a bulletin board to post notes, praises, and positive comments about each other. Tell them this is what you expect them to do and they'll do it.

- And, of course... yourself!

Schedule time in your planner and week to call distant offices or individuals and genuinely ask how things are going. Offer help and communication on things that may not have filtered down.

Send all head office communications *immediately* by courier if lateness has created negative perceptions.

Follow up on communications; write down in your contact management systems, PDA or planner to touch base on agreed reviews of process, conversations and assignments.

Yes, you may have to use phone and e-mail to do most of this but remember to schedule field trips to their locations once in a while. Do this quarterly if possible, semi-annually as a minimum.

Even schedule the occasional meeting in their neck of the woods versus at head office.

Go Get'em Giving Ideas

1. Just imagine if you were in a distant location removed from head office, what would tick you off most that you missed out on? What would you like to see happen that would make you feel valued and appreciated? Apply this to your current field workers and find out how their perspective is similar or different to yours.

2. Get senior leaders involved. Where the rapport is positive bring a senior leader out to the field at least once a year. Staff love this opportunity to connect with company leaders. Make sure it is casual and the leader has a chance to converse with staff (we've had comments on this one).

43.

GREETINGS AND SOLICITATIONS

Do you take time to greet your employees and peers?

Informal surveys through employee interviews in the companies and organizations I consult indicate a growing trend that managers and supervisors hardly ever greet or even acknowledge employees.

Here I am talking about the pleasantries of "good morning," "hi" and "see you tomorrow" at the end of the day. Add the person's name on the end and you have it made.

To management's defense, both they and employees are facing ever increasing workload and balance demands. Sometimes, coming up for air is challenging enough.

One organization took this issue to heart and had a group of their managers plan to make time to greet employees on a consistent basis.

What was the result from doing this action? Read the following outcomes and see if they don't provide you with some practical Real Recognition™ giving tips.

There was surprise on the managers' part as to the positive, appreciated, and morale boosting impact this simple act had on employees. They never realized how much personal contact meant to their own employees.

Check out some of these benefits that managers' accrued from taking just a small amount of time to do what seemed like such a small action:

- Finding out what employees are actually working on from a genuine interest perspective and not a "Big Brother" and critical evaluator mindset.
- Created an opportunity to actually talk with employees who sometimes were missed in the everyday life at work.
- Employees became much more comfortable in talking to management and sharing their feelings.
- Having employees share more of their world with managers, both personal and professional.
- More positive relationships were formed and this helped develop greater trust.

Go Get'em Giving Ideas

1. Take stock of how you are doing. Make sure you are not letting job demands and workload pressures get in the way of a friendly greeting and smile. For the week coming up, plan on a daily basis to be a genuine, positive greeter of your employees and peers.

2. Now while you do this, make a note of the reactions from colleagues and employees. How did they change by the end of the week? What were the benefits you gained from this simple action?

44.

KNOWING WHAT IS IMPORTANT

A key skill in Giving the Real Recognition Way is knowing what's important to each of your employees.

In Joe Callowa's great customer service book "Becoming a Category of One" he outlines Three Rules for customers which are as follows:

Rule 1: Know more about the customer than anyone else.
Rule 2: Get closer to the customer than anyone else.
Rule 3: Emotionally connect with the customer better than anyone else.

I have seen a corollary set of rules that apply to the treatment of employees in giving them Real Recognition™. In my mind Real Recognition™ occurs when you follow these rules:

Rule 1: Know Them Well
Rule 2: Build Positive Relationships
Rule 3: Show Caring Concern

Know Them Well

You may have spent a lot of time profiling your clients and customers. Often it is for business and monetary outcomes, but hopefully you are doing it to show genuine interest in the individual. .

Similarly, you should make time to record pertinent details about each employee and over time accumulate interesting details, the little things, about knowing each employee.

Workforce.com writer, Eve Tahmincioglu, wrote in an article entitled "Gifts That Gall" about a top producer of an insurance company repeatedly earned the top salesperson distinction and who just stopped attending all award ceremonies.

Noting the salesperson's absence, the sales manager had to ask themselves the question, "What is really important to this individual?" Do you know what was most important to this particular salesperson? It was his wife and his three daughters. The result of asking this question was that the following year the company gave this repeat top salesperson a portrait of his family. The gesture was greatly appreciated.

Build Positive Relationships

Building a positive relationship takes active listening and making time for each employee. It takes self-discipline and a philosophy of one of my recognition rules "Relationships first, tasks second."

When you add up the time for most employee interactions they usually amount to a very small number of minutes. Put relationship building actions in your "to do" list and prioritize them ahead of the tasks. That pile of paperwork, inbox of e-mails, and projects will *always* be there. People will not.

Show Caring Concern

It is always the little things that count the most.

Following up after a medical test to see how things are with an employee. Asking how the baseball finals went after a weekend for one of your staff's children. Noticing non-verbal behaviors that show something is not quite right and asking them how they are *really* doing.

And it's leaving cards, notes, even Post-It® Notes expressing appreciation for them and the job they are doing. Little things like accompanying a thank you note with their favorite chocolate bar or treat or drink (which you have determined during your investigating time in finding out personal information).

Go Get'em Giving Ideas

1. Relationships first, Tasks second. Review how you prioritize your "to do" lists in your electronic organizers or planners. Are you putting "things" ahead of people? Try timing how long personal interactions actually take. You'll find they range from seconds to just a few minutes. The return on investment is always far greater for the small amount of time it really takes.

2. Develop employee profiles. This is not a spying mindset. Use genuine interest and ask them directly as well as being a keen observer. Don't hesitate to ask others. Personalize your recognition giving with this wealth of information that will demonstrate meaning and genuine care.

45.

NOTHING TO RECOGNIZE?

During a recent company seminar session a participant questioned, "what if there is nothing to recognize?" My reply evolved around three key areas:

1. Find Things to Recognize

Do you know the complete role of your employees? Do you understand what it takes to complete a task, the interruptions, problems, and systems involved? Are you interacting regularly with your employees to know how *they* are doing as well as *what* they are doing? What about scheduling one-on-one time once a month to just talk and to give and receive feedback?

Be out there observing and learning about people and their jobs. In order to catch people doing things right, you have to go out and play catch.

2. Encourage Positive Performances

There is no doubt there will always be some employees who will never rise to be the shining stars of your workplace. Yet they show up faithfully, perform often mundane, repetitive tasks day in and day out, and don't complain.

These life-blood people of the company need to be encouraged in what they are doing. Simply thank them for their consistent work performance, arriving on time everyday, the good quality of their work. Just because it is not above and beyond behavior does not mean you should simply ignore giving them recognition for what they do.

Employees always want to be recognized for what they do.

3. Create Growth Opportunities

And for the reality answer check, what are you doing to create growth opportunities for our employees. Even if some job functions are repetitive, are you finding out what your employees want to do in the immediate and long-term future? Do you even know what their personal dreams and goals are?

Are there special projects they would like to take on? Is there a chance for some cross-training so occasional change of job functioning can be arranged? What education or work goals do they want to work on?

By creating a new experience you will easily find something to recognize.

Remember the perception that there is nothing to recognize lies fully with the supervisor or manager to find, encourage and grow performance opportunities that *can* be appreciated.

Go Get'em Giving Ideas

1. Achievement Logs. Take the load off of yourself for always finding and observing. Develop an online or hard copy form for employees to record their achievements on a monthly basis. Visit with them monthly or bi-monthly and learn first-hand of their individual successes. You'll be amazed and they'll appreciate the sit-down opportunity to share.

2. Staff Meetings. These need not always be the once-a-month formal kind of meeting. Sometimes, all you need is the before work quickie meeting that can be an excellent chance for group and individual acknowledgement of great things going on. With the more formal staff meetings make sure there is always recognition time on the agenda. Don't leave a meeting without a recognition opportunity!

46.

GET RID OF THE MONEY

A recent question posed at a presentation this week was, "What do you do when after a year of giving recognition, at the end of the year the people say, 'now show me the money?'"

The answer to this, and a practical recognition tip to hang onto, is: "Get rid of the money."

1. Pay People Fairly

The first reason people tend to focus on money for is when they have not been paid fairly. Do whatever you can to get the pay structure and performance management in place to ensure pay increments and performance increases are done fairly and on time. Make sure there are good benefits and do a regular review of the compensation system.

2. Stop Focusing On The Money

When paid well, the culture of the organization needs to remove the emphasis on money. People need to know the visionary culture of the organization is purposeful. Profits then become the outcome of a meaningful workplace. So work on making the values and vision the top focus. Work on purpose.

Go Get'em Giving Ideas

1. Find out employee satisfaction levels. From a recent survey we conducted, 92 percent of managers indicated recognition strongly impacts employee satisfaction levels. When you do your next survey, find out whether your workplace is purpose driven or money driven.

2. Keep competitive on pay. It is so important to ensure your salaries and pay structure are competitive. Pay the market rate. If you can't pay more, how are you going to be better in other areas, such as benefits and services provided? Other things can offset for slightly lower pay. Ask your employees what they would like to see you provide.

47.

POSITIVE ATTENTION

Suzanne Wintrob in an article entitled "Reward A Job Well Done" in the Financial Post (May 10, 2004) wrote about the value of both listening and giving within the workplace.

These two critical actions can be grouped under the heading "positive attention."

Positive attention is strongly needed, according to this article, if you are to continue to enhance productivity. Technology has been well utilized and invested in, but you have to give positive attention to engage the people you work with.

Susan Heathfield, a human resources specialist, wrote in her article on "The Power of Positive Recognition" about four simple steps to show Positive Attention. Notice how the acts of listening and giving are implied in each of them:

1. Stop by an individual's workstation or office to talk informally.
2. Provide frequent positive performance feedback – at least weekly.
3. Provide public praise at a staff meeting.
4. Take an employee out to lunch.

The accumulation effect of positive attention is tremendous. So please…Pay positive attention!

Go Get'em Giving Ideas

1. Get a piece of paper and make two columns with the headings "listening" and "giving." Now write down 10 things you can do under each column to demonstrate listening and

giving. Randomly choose one and go out and put it into practice.

2. Do a positive attention audit. Even with your own list ask yourself how are *you* doing? Where do you need to improve? How are other managers and leaders modeling these actions? Now bring this up in a management meeting and have each manager do his or her own self-appraisal. Should make for some interesting discussion afterwards!

48.

MEMORABLE CONNECTIONS

Whatever recognition/awards programs or activities you have going on you have to keep them top of mind in your employees' minds as well as for your managers.

In preparing a presentation for the Scotiabank inTek group I learned they had developed specific award categories playing on the "inTek" company name. For example, they have awards such as "inTune" for customer service, "inSync" for teamwork and "inSight" for innovation. That is what I call good linkage!

These branding concepts allow for greater connection as well as buy in from the employees so long as everything else is done correctly. It becomes an opportunity for maximizing Giving the Real Recognition Way.

Other organizations like Duke University have used acronyms or acrostics to use a meaningful word and mold it to their own award areas.

Duke's THANKS program works the word "Thanks" into:
- **T**eamwork
- **H**ospitality
- **A**ttendance
- i**N**dividual effort
- **K**nowledge
- **S**ervice

Even with the creative license for the "n" in "thanks" the Duke folks there are going to remember this awards program.

So allow the name to become a memorable and positive connection for your awards and recognition program.

Go Get'em Giving Ideas

1. Branding opportunity. Is there a way to use your company name or key products in the name of your recognition initiatives? Work with your communications and your marketing departments on suggestions. *Always* run these suggestions by employees afterwards and have them grade or rank order preferences.

2. Acronyms and acrostics are a wonderful stand by when stuck for a name. What is it you want to focus on? Is there a key principle, idea or message that needs to be reinforced? Remember, you can always "borrow" and simply rework the words in the acronym.

49.

CREATING SPONTANEITY

Trending specialists at "Trendwatching.com" have dubbed a recent consumer trend for making spontaneous decisions to go somewhere or do something as "planned spontaneity." Apparently it is becoming the norm; often the only thing consumers are willing to plan for is to actually be... spontaneous!

One easy problem to fall into with doing employee recognition is to make it so planned and orchestrated that it doesn't seem *real* anymore. So try the tip of being more spontaneous.

To correct this rigid recognition it might be worthwhile to do some planned spontaneous strategy development with your employee recognition programs.

The solution is to be more spontaneous with giving recognition. "Spontaneity: defined as *[n] the quality of being spontaneous and coming from natural feelings without constraint.*"

This is learning to be both creative and immediate in channeling your feelings towards appreciating those around you.

- Spelling out the word "THANKS" with M&M's or favorite piece-sized candies on a person's desk.
- Actually stopping work for 10-15 minutes for a randomly selected opportunity and bring out the milk and cookies to eat.
- Making a hand made thank you card using only items in the office (could be quite interesting or very artistic!).

- Going outside on a hot day and having slushies (flavored crushed ice drinks) or popsicles.
- Writing a poem or turning it into a song to express your appreciation for someone

Go Get'em Giving Ideas

1. Challenge yourself to be more spontaneous. This doesn't come naturally to me either if you're even wondering. *But...* I have to say that within my marriage with dates and activities with the kids I have *purposely* challenged myself to do the impromptu stuff. (Imagine a date of going to a Lazy-boy store and trying out all the massage chairs and frustrating the salespeople with no sale!)

2. Read creativity books. There are now tons on the bookshelves from Edward de Bono to Roger von Oech and even Doug Hall's latest works. Dig in and mine out what you can apply to your attempts at *planned spontaneous* employee recognition.

50.

CONFORMING TO INDIVIDUALITY

Have you noticed the way kids dress or groom themselves these days, and even adults for that matter? Many want to stand out as individuals.

I see this one woman regularly walking the city streets on her way to work who has pink hair. Now that's her prerogative and I have nothing against pink or any other colored hair. The irony is within a week you can find someone else with pink hair as well.

Same thing exists with recognition. My observation and research shows that people want to be recognized as individuals and not just part of the crowd. The neat thing is that while you may recognize one person's individual efforts and accomplishments, someone else will have similar achievements *or* want to be recognized in the same way.

By offering more choice in the kinds of awards or gifts being given you will find out there are others who want the same things too.

This is what I call conforming individuality and can be a helpful tip in your awards selection.

Take this example from the public sector research we conducted (see *Public Personnel Management* Vol. 33, No. 3, Fall 2004).

Canadian public service managers show a higher preference for having logo and other identifiers of their organization on their awards (56%) than their U.S. counterparts (44%).

Similarly, Canadian managers indicated a greater desire (70%) for more lifestyle related awards than managers in the U.S. (55%). Notice the conformity of many people wanting to be recognized individually.

While the survey was not designed to identify the reasons, none of us can pretend to know the rationale for the above differences. The fact is they do exist.

So take advantage of noting the repeated cases of individuality in the workplace. They just may help with your recognition efforts. Even pink hair!

Go Get'em Giving Ideas

1. Fact finding expedition. Ask employees the kind of awards and gifts they would prefer. You may want to survey past recipients for their input and employees in general through an online or paper survey. You may be amazed at the possibilities. So find out what individuals want and conform!

2. Work with your supplier. Many awards and recognition providers are creating many more options for employees to select from. They can customize a catalog to include company logo embossed awards or heritage based items and clothing, as well as more lifestyle items for employees to choose from. Individualize your awards.

51.

ASK WHAT MOTIVATES

So many times I am asked, "What is the best kind of recognition to give to employees?" Of course the answer always has to be, "That depends."

Let's look at three tips to finding out what is it that motivates an employee so you can be Giving the Real Recognition Way.

- Take time to ask. You have to create opportunities for informal discussions and find out about their goals, ambitions, motivations, likes and dislikes, their fears and dreams. Such information is a gold mine once you have gleaned it. You can also respectfully ask others who are close to that individual.

- Take time to listen. You have to be all ears on and off the job. It is amazing what you can discover through the casual conversations in order to determine people's passions and interests.

- Take time to observe. Always be on the lookout and notice what people read, photos displayed of family and friends, memorabilia and items in the office, where and what they like to eat, all add to the data you need to understand a person's true motivations.

Putting this all together helps you better appreciate what a person likes to do and what they are good at. Knowing these factors of what they like and what they are good at are key motivation points.

Go Get'em Giving Ideas

1. Create an employee character sketch. Write up a paragraph describing everything you can about each employee so that someone new reading your notes could identify them from your notes. Note their likes and dislikes, their qualities, talents, hobbies, etc. Once you are done your character sketch you will have a better recollection of each employee that will help you when searching for recognition ideas.

2. A little bit them and a little bit you. Personally I am doing my holiday party gift shopping around the personal traits of my colleagues along with some of our own talents and abilities. That way we get them something that shows what we think and know about them along with something that is meaningful from us personally.

52.

HOW DOES IT SOUND?

Here's an interesting test for you to see how "real" the recognition giving currently going on in your organization really is. You can either evaluate acts of recognition by direct observation and acts of listening in, or by simply asking recognition recipients the question, "How did the recognition you received 'sound' to you?"

Dig deeper with questions like the following:

- Was it genuine?
- Did it sound hollow?
- Was it sincere?
- Were you happy with what you heard said?
- Did it sound right?
- Do you recall the words that were said?
- Have you told others what was said to you?

A clear indicator of the success of how the recognition sounds is in the last question: Telling others what was said. When the praise and appreciation action starts becoming one of the "telling stories" where you work you know it was "said right." Then you know people are Giving the Real Recognition Way.

Go Get'em Giving Ideas

1. Sounding board practice. Before giving someone some recognition just take a minute to think through what you will say. It does not have to be so scripted that it sounds artificial. Just remember to be specific about what was done, use the person's name, and tell them how their action made a difference to you and the company.

2. Start making an audio log of the recognition you hear spoken where you work. Evaluate how it sounds. If you are in a management or supervisory position it may be appropriate to give feedback to the giver to acknowledge what they said or to provide concrete coaching feedback to them.

53.

THE CUTE FACTOR

In speaking with an acquaintance this week, I described one group's award to her. It was simply an old sports award with some figurine on top. Somebody put it on a colleague's desk with a little hand made sash around the body that had printed on it something like, "The Best Organized Person I Know." A note was left with the award instructing the recipient to pass it on to someone else and customize a new sash with some other descriptive praise and acknowledgement.

The acquaintance I spoke with described this award as simply "cute" and she really liked it.

So what makes an award or a recognition action become classified as "cute."

In checking out the dictionary I found the following meanings for the word "cute."

1. Delightfully pretty or dainty
2. Obviously contrived to charm; precious
3. Shrewd; clever

Cute was originally a shortened form of acute in the sense of being "keenly perceptive or discerning, shrewd."

Based on these qualities and attributes you can look at the recognition you are going to give and ask does it pass the "cute factor."

By being keenly perceptive and discerning of an individual's likes and dislikes, wants and needs, desires and aspirations, you should gain oodles of ideas of what to give a person to acknowledge their contributions.

So the next time you hear someone say, "that's cute," analyze and dissect the ingredients that made it *cute*. Learn from it and replicate it.

Go Get'em Giving Ideas

1. Remember cuteness is in the eye of the beholder. Yet advertisers marketing many personal care items and other products have done painstaking research to know what would appeal to consumers. In profiling their customers they learn a great deal. What can you learn about your employees?

2. I like the term, "contrived to charm." By finding out information about your employees you can contrive, if you will, the very genuine feelings you want to leave behind with them through what you give someone that would charm them.

54.

QUICK HITS CAN BE A GOOD QUICK FIX

Acting right away on simple, doable and realistic goals will pay dividends no matter what industry you are in. This can be an essential tip for Giving the Real Recognition Way. By acting immediately to recognize quick successes or innovative ideas you can acknowledge the contributions employees make when they share how things can be improved, for example.

Work carried out in the hospitality industry by Jonathan Barsky, Jan McDougal and Cindi Frame of Market Metrix LLC, provides good demonstration of what happens when you act fast upon employee survey results.

According to a report in Hotel & Motel Management, the authors indicate that implementation of "quick hits" or immediate action on identified issues or concerns can make a *big* difference on satisfaction scores.

These "quick hits" reportedly also play a critical role in demonstrating management's commitment to taking action.

Tom Chamberlain, general manager at the Affinia Dumont in New York increased one component of his hotel's satisfaction score by 15 points by working with associates to conduct inventory twice a month instead of once a month.

Joe Root, general manager of The Lodge at CordeValle in San Martin, California, discovered by staying overnight just once a month, he was able to reconnect with night shift employees, and raised his overall employee satisfaction score six points in just six months (source: www.hotelmotel.com   ).

Too many times employee satisfaction surveys are carried out but with no action based on employee input.

Remember there are such things as "good" quick fixes.

Go Get'em Giving Ideas

1. If you have survey results to draw upon, do so. If not, get a focus group representing a good cross-section of employees at all levels. Now identify the top three issues employees feel should be improved. Next identify *one* action that could be achieved on one of these top three items which would demonstrate things can be changed.

2. Make a *simple* action plan. Round up a team of 7 to 9 employees including a facilitator leader. Now go and make things happen. The idea is to improve or solve the problem within 90-days. Meet together once every 30-day cycle and give weekly e-mail or phone reports on every action step taken.

55.

PEOPLE WATCHING

Do you make time to re-read or peruse the books on your shelf?

I am going through my copy of Robert K. Cooper's book "The Other 90%" again which looks at unlocking the vast untapped potential we have for leadership and life.

Those of you who know my approach to employee recognition are aware that we all need to improve our awareness of what those around us do that merits acknowledgement and praise.

Cooper suggests we need to use a day book or notebook and start noting observations of say 3 or 4 people who are actually important to us.

Ask yourself these questions as a key to your observations:

- What stands out about them?
- Were there any gifts or talents that you saw used?
- When do you see them getting excited?
- What makes their eyes light up?
- What do you see that is important to them?

Naturally, when you see things that are exemplary, you have a great opportunity to express your appreciation for those qualities and actions displayed. You can say something like, "I couldn't help noticing that…."and fill in the blanks with a captured observation. Of course you would be right because you have been in the act of "noticing" them.

So become a keen observer of the people you work with and take note of all they do that merits recognition in your eyes.

Go Get'em Giving Ideas

1. Notebook notices. Try this out for just one week. Get a notebook and record answers to the questions stated in this chapter as you find out the answers. This will truly help you to sharpen your observation skills. Make sure you have this as a "to do" task in your Palm, BlackBerry or day planner so you make a regular habit of doing this.

2. After you have tried this with people who are important to you (certainly a more rewarding connection), start adding a person who may not be well known to you.

Example: I have made time to tell receptionists on the phone that I have to repeatedly speak with, how well they do their job and often ask for their names so I can address the "unknown" person in a more personable manner.

56.

IMMEDIATE RECOGNITION, PLEASE

In our area the Shell company gas service stations have an automatic pay system you can apply for. You receive a key tag with a personal bar code that debits your credit card and credits your loyalty awards account.

I get a thrill out of placing my key tag on the black rectangle visible on the pumps that scans and reads it and immediately displays the bold lettered and flashing sign, "RECOGNIZED."

You can understand with my focus on employee recognition that I really like the immediacy of this response… and at the same time not having to remove my wallet!

Recognition takes little or no time at all to give and the sooner it is given the more meaningful it becomes.

As soon as you observe or hear an employee providing exceptional performance go right away and "tag" them, if you will, with a simple 1, 2, 3 approach:

1. Verbal praise and acknowledgement.
2. Specific description of the actions being praised.
3. Telling them why it meant so much to you.

Then stand back and watch that employee light up as if the word "RECOGNIZED" was printed on their forehead.

Go Get'em Giving Ideas

1. Take time practicing in giving immediate recognition. Not all of us are born praisers and recognizers. I know I am not. Even if it does not come naturally to you, the art and practice

can be learned. Just follow the 1, 2, 3 approach outlined above and start looking out for store and hotel clerks to get a handle on saying things right. The more comfortable you become with people you do not work with the easier it will be with those you associate with in the workplace on a regular basis.

2. Resist procrastinating recognition giving. Don't put off recognizing exceptional contributions. Even if you find it hard to do, start getting motivated by the great feelings you'll start receiving for making someone else feel good about themselves and their work

57.

INSTILLING PRIDE AT WORK

In his exceptional book, "Why Pride Matters More Than Money," Jon Katzenbach identifies three simple strategies for managers to hang their hats on which will be great focus points for Giving the Real Recognition Way.

First is to always have your compass set on "pride."

In other words, pride is an ongoing journey and experience and is not an endpoint destination. It is something one experiences and managers must continually orchestrate. So the goal is to stimulate emotional commitment to the work and contributions employees make on a daily basis.

Second is to localize as much as possible.

I see this issue as a critical piece. Recognition and pride is always observed at the local or micro level. We can never expect or wait for the company as a whole or for senior leaders alone to instill it. It's the manager or supervisor right above you and the peers along side of you who help instill pride and reinforce it for one another.

Third is to integrate multiple sources of pride around a few simple messages.

Katzenbach's approach is to keep things simple, focused and uncomplicated. Managers must find a narrowed set of leading indicators to focus and acknowledge workers on. While there are always the multiple company key indicators a good leader narrows these factors down to the most important one or two to hammer on and praise.

And it is the sharing and retelling of the marvelous "going the extra mile" stories that become the examples for others to be able to follow.

Go Get'em Giving Ideas

1. Always remember that Real Recognition™ is a feeling. Instilling pride in the workplace is a constant, consistent practice of stating and reminding what an organization values.

2. Another set of three's for you. Pride can be associated with these three factors: people, products and performance. What one thing can you do to instill greater pride in any of those three areas?

58.

WHAT EMPLOYEES WANT

Many of us have seen the listings of the top 50 or 100 employers that the Hay Group works on each year. They help remind us of the need to constantly meshing wants versus needs with Giving the Real Recognition Way.

With the Hay Group they have created the term which they call "Engaged Performance™," and nicely identifies six core areas to categorize most employees' wants, namely:

- *Inspiration and values:* this addresses all aspects of identifying, communicating and consistent living of good, meaningful values by everyone in an organization.

- *Future growth and opportunity:* looks at career and personal development opportunities as well as feedback on individual performance

- *Work-life balance:* here they look at how people know they are cared for and that home and community are also important along with work related goals and performance.

- *Tangible rewards:* refers to compensation and rewards such as fair pay, appropriate bonuses, benefits and incentives for work performed.

- *Quality of work:* work is examined as to whether employees perceive it as meaningful, challenging and interesting as well as balanced with respect to workload along with positive collegial interaction

- *Enabling environment:* refers to the physical environment along with the right tools, training and safety being in place.

These six areas tend to lean more towards a reward paradigm or strategy versus recognition per se. But I still think it is important to examine these factors in any workplace. They are all contributing pieces to making recognition giving a part of the Real Recognition™ way you do things.

Go Get'em Giving Ideas

1. Keep things transparent. Employees must never feel rewards are used as a manipulation technique. Consultation with employees and managers is critical in knowing what employees *really* want. At the same time those responsible for employee recognition must always balance out wants versus the program purposes and budget.

2. Follow the winds of change. What employees want will and does change over time. Managers need to continually keep apprised of current management research and findings. It is important to understand the principles and theories of what motivates people and to constantly be on the lookout for emerging trends in employee wants.

59.

STUART LITTLE APPROACH

My wife hates the animated "Stuart Little" movies. She can't stand animated, real-to-life, talking animals...especially when it's a mouse!

But there is a lot to learn from being little. For one thing you get to see the little things in life in a big way which you may generally take for granted. Being much bigger than a mouse we tend to look only at the large things in life. We miss a great deal this way. Apply this thought when you are Giving the Real Recognition Way.

That's why I love the Estonian proverb, "Who does not thank for little will not thank for much." If we don't stop to thank for the little things we'll never stop to thank people for the big things they do.

So think little. Stop and smell the roses. Get a magnifying glass if you have to and start finding the little things to praise.

Go Get'em Giving Ideas

1. Little things in life. Try this at home if you have a partner/spouse and/or family. Find one little thing each person does in a day or week that you take for granted and have never said anything about. Express your appreciation to them for what they do. Do it tonight.

2. Little things at work. I once started leaving different worded notes for our office assistant on items to be photocopied. I always used unique ways of expressing my appreciation, from "gracias" to "danke" and all the great ways of glitzing up a

Post-It® Note. An unexpected benefit from this small gesture was my photocopying always ended up getting done first!

60.

UNDER THE INFLUENCE

No, I am not talking about alcohol!!

I am speaking of the numerous people who have influenced you and me to be successful in life.

Have you stopped to reflect on the people who have made you who you are today? Imagine if each of us stopped and made time to thank someone in writing and expressed our sincere appreciation for the difference they have made in our lives. Think how giving thanks the Real Recognition™ way to these great influencers would impact the world.

I read a magazine article once about a group of men who had reflected together on people who had influenced their lives. In talking about these individuals they decided to express their gratitude to them by locating them and writing a letter of thanks. One man remembered a high school teacher who had introduced him to the literary works of Tennyson. He made the time that day to sit down and write a letter to thank her.

A while later he received an unexpected, written reply back from the teacher. While the handwriting was more of a feeble scrawl, she expressed how much his note had meant to her. This once vibrant high school teacher was now in her 80's and she was living alone. She told this former student how she had taught school for 50 years and that his was the first note of appreciation she had ever received. The note had arrived at a low point in her life, on a blue and cold morning, and had cheered her up as nothing had done in years.

This story may feel particularly relevant whenever it's time to get your own children ready to return to school.

And no matter when in our lives, we all need to reflect on who has influenced us in our lives and take time out to express our gratitude to them. Otherwise they may never know.

Go Get'em Giving Ideas

1. Make a list of the people who have influenced you in your life. I once wrote Dr. Norman Vincent Peale and thanked him for his powerful book, *"The Power of Positive Thinking."* I never expected a reply but received a letter back from him *and* a signed copy of his latest book. Those who truly give from the heart seem to just keep giving.

2. With your list now made, write one of those people this week. Do it today if you can. If possible make time to write one person a week from your list and express your sincere appreciation for the influence they have made on your life. Your note may be a turning point in someone's life.

61.

WANTED!!

I haven't watched a good ol' fashioned Western movie in a long time. But I do remember the classic "WANTED" posters for the villain or glorified gunslinger that would be displayed on the sheriffs' jail wall.

There was always a high dollar amount for the reward for capturing the person. Perhaps there is a learning point here we can benefit from in Giving the Real Recognition Way.

Employees are trying to raise "wanted" signs of their own right where you work. They want you to acknowledge their involvement on the job, the great ideas they willingly share, the sacrifice for staying late, and all the qualities that add up to their contribution in the workplace. They want their reward!

By capturing their hearts and minds and recognizing them for it, your employees will reward you immensely whether in loyalty or outstanding performance.

So look out for posted and not so visible "WANTED" signs where you work.

Go Get'em Giving Ideas

1. Some of the "wanted" posters you'll find in the cafeteria or by the water cooler. They won't be actual signs but words spoken in informal gatherings and conversations. Take note. They are tracks which will lead you to improving employee motivation.

2. Work from the opposite angle. What would be your reward for having great morale, and a highly motivated and

competitive workplace? You have identified the reward amount on your poster. Now you must ask yourself, "What are you willing to give in return for this?" Brainstorm with your management team the actions you must take to capture the hearts and minds of your employees.

Section 3

9 Career-Crushing Mistakes to Avoid

62.

TRICK OR TREAT?

I think I know what some employees go through and what happens with some recognition initiatives in many companies.

Have you ever experienced or seen this? See if you can relate to it and at the same time learn what it takes to prevent this recognition mistake from happening to you.

In North America we have a commercially influenced and fun annual event called Halloween each October 31st. Children, and sometimes older youth, dress up as goblins, ghosts and various movie and cartoon characters, go door to door with bag in hand, and receive candy and other treats after saying, "Trick or treat!"

Past tradition suggested each homeowner could ask the child at their door to perform a trick to earn the treat.

These days there is more of an attitude of entitlement to just receive the candy without even a word being spoken.

Similarly, employers and employees can fall into the same trap of entitlement philosophy with rewards and recognition. They just want the treat, please and thank you.

How do you stop this entitlement mindset? Try to set specific, measurable criteria for earning recognition. This would be the equivalent of performing the trick. Be consistent with the expectation. It then becomes the standard to reach for.

If the plaques or monetary incentives or whatever recognition is given is not tied to some performance expectation you'll actually create a backfiring of some trick, so to speak, by your employees. These tricks may take on the shape of tardiness, poor productivity, negative communication, and cynicism. These are all just some of the possible outcomes from an entitlement philosophy around recognition.

So be careful that the goodies you give out at the office door are only given for great performances.

Go Get'em Giving Ideas

1. Performing the Trick. Performance expectations must be clearly established and clearly communicated. Once you have that done you pave the way for employees to deliver great on-the-job tricks worthy of the treats you have provided.

2. Right kind of Treats. I sit with an "Oh Henry!" mini-chocolate bar on my computer desk. My daughter just brought this down when I was writing this. She knows what I like. It is meaningful to *me*. Make sure what you reward your employees with is meaningful to them or your supposed treat will turn sour!

63.

IT'S BONUS TIME?

So how many companies still give the traditional annual bonus at the end of the year? And... are they really a *bonus*? Or do they unintentionally become a recognition mistake?

According to an online reader survey through Workforce Magazine (November 2005, 727 respondents) the following insights were identified:

- 48% We give annual cash bonuses
- 48% These bonuses are performance-based
- 25% We do not give annual bonuses
- 22% These bonuses are across the board
- 9% We give both stock-based and cash bonuses
- 4% We gave annual cash bonuses at one time, but have discontinued them
- 2% We give stock-based annual bonuses
- 1% We gave annual stock-based awards at one time, but have discontinued

Just under half of the employer respondents still give out cash bonuses to employees and it appears they are closely performance based rather than just the "here's your bonus" scenario. Less than 10 percent give stocks and cash.

From the Hewitt Associates' 2005 holiday survey fifty-five percent of company respondents have eliminated holiday bonus programs because of cost, and 50 percent explained this was because of the growing "entitlement philosophy," which I talked about in the previous chapter. In this case, the Hewitt survey did not necessarily refer to cash.

To get rid of the entitlement philosophy I agree with the need for some kind of performance measure that warrants whether "yea" or "nay" to giving a bonus to someone, or some variation of set amounts per performance measure.

Finally, take time to make sure there is some written or verbal acknowledgement accompanying the bonus. Don't let it just sit there on a check or with the bills. Give it a personal touch. Tell them how much you appreciate their efforts.

Go Get'em Giving Ideas

1. Clip the bonus. My brainstorm for giving actual hard cold cash would be to give a logo engraved money clip along with the simple word, *"Thanks"* engraved on it as well. See how that would warm up the money!

2. Positive connection. Bonus time could be a wonderful time to have another one-on-one chat with your employees on their performance, or on their goals for the New Year, along with a genuine expression of good wishes and concern for them and their family members.

64.

OBLIGATION OR CELEBRATION?

I wanted to share some seasonal learning points I gained following a Christmas or end of year holiday season and the principles learned behind the actions. This should help prevent a major recognition mistake!

On my way back from Montreal, the December 16, 2005 Globe and Mail newspaper displayed the results of an online survey where they asked the following question, "Does your employer throw a party to celebrate the holiday season?"

Now the available answer statements to select from were as follows, and the results revealed their respective percentages:

- 32% - Yes, we have a big blowout that everyone enjoys
- 21% - No party – my employer is a Scrooge
- 16% - Yes, it's big, but more of an obligation than a celebration
- 16% - Yes, but it's getting more modest each year
- 16% - Yes, but it's done on the cheap. What a joke!

My evaluation from these numbers was to make sure you don't do such events out of "Obligation" but truly make it a "Celebration." By making their party celebration events *truly* a celebration the percentage of high yeses with enjoyment could have risen by another 32 percent!

Look at the emotions and feelings that the word "obligation" conjures up. It's chore-like, boring, un-fun. Now, contrast that with the mood and experience of having a "celebration." This would bring excitement, enjoyment, togetherness, and many more adjectives. Quite the difference!

I can look at my bookshelf and see even the subtitle of a great book to provide the solution. Terrence Deal and M.K. Key's book, *"Corporate Celebration"* has the subtitle of "Play, Purpose and Profit at Work."

So to turn your awards events from Obligation to Celebration just add the ingredients of *play* and *purpose*. The irony is that Profits at Work will always be the outcome.

Go Get'em Giving Ideas

1. PURPOSE. Never hold *any* event without a purpose. Achievement of goals for the year and hard work together or building unity can be just some of the reasons. A party should be a great way to *truly* say thank you! So remember that for next year's party!

2. PLAY. We all know that all work and no play make Jack and Jill dull! Deal and Key further highlight in their book that to make play happen you have to delight, bring in surprise, and create release. This can be a release of tension, fostering creativity and bonding a group together. Bring in more surprises for the New Year!

65.

VIRTUAL REALITY

Many people are asking questions around virtual recognition today because of the growing virtual workforce. The Workforce e-newsletter also highlighted this issue. Understanding this virtual reality will help you from making an unforgivable recognition mistake.

In a report by Lily Mok from the research firm Gartner from Stamford, Connecticut, she wrote: "Practices such as 'management by walking around' can no longer be applied to managing a virtual workforce. Because virtual workers are 'out-of-sight' of their managers, they tend to become 'out-of-mind' over time," a circumstance that hurts morale, cuts down on productivity and hinders employee performance. The chief challenge lies in "how to effectively manage and lead individuals into cohesive, high-performing teams in a virtual workplace setting."

There is a mix of issues here:

1. Hiring the right kind of person to be a virtual worker.

2. Managing differently and thereby giving recognition differently.

Virtual workers need high involvement and empowerment to make decisions. They need to be close to the business processes in order to make those decisions without relying on a manager. They must be proactive on their own personal and professional development. They must be flexible, fast and focused on the goals of the company.

Guidelines for Managers of Virtual Employees

- *Do more with what you do the least*

For example: when you do make a face-to-face visit, take more time than you would at head office. Even make it a luncheon visit and thereby build the relationship everyone at the office takes for granted. Stay a while rather than the fleeting walk through and disappearing into meetings.

- *Give more lead time to virtual employees*

Suggestion: Send notices of meetings, teleconferences, etc. a few days earlier than those at head office. That way you deflect the attitude and often the reality that everyone at head office hears about things first. Why not start an important announcement over the phone with the virtual staff before the face-to-face meeting at head office.

- *Communicate frequently and with variety*

Idea: Send more personal e-mails versus the typical task oriented ones. Leave a recognition telephone message before the day starts or after they have gone, praising them for a job well done. Those kinds of messages get "saved" for a while. Send your virtual workers post-cards from your travels and give a boosting message. Why not record an mp3 message and send it to them.

Go Get'em Giving Ideas

1. Why not apply Long Distant Grand-parenting techniques. We frequently send cards and gifts to our grandchildren that are a perfect fit for each child. Be on the lookout for unique

items to send a perfect message to your virtual employees. It will show them you care.

2. Put more of *you* into what you send. We have bought Winnie the Pooh books for our grandchildren and I have read and recorded the books on tape using my best rendition of the character voices. Imagine capturing a speech you give to your staff that is recorded and sent to all your virtual employees.

66.

TAKE TIME

Yep, this recognition giving tip will make you the king or queen where you work, and in life in general. To not do it at all will make you the king or queen of recognition mistakes.

Take time: to get to know the ward clerk on a hospital floor where a loved one is. You'll never know when you may need help beyond the doctor.

Take time: to thank a receptionist with using their name for helping you with needed information. They could open the doors for whatever you need in the future.

Take time: to thank your manager for the way they gave you some needed feedback. You will get more positive feedback along the way.

Take time: to write a thank you card for someone who went out of their way to set things up for you. You might hear how it made their day.

Take time: to write a letter to someone who made a difference to you. I once received a signed copy of a book from the noted author Dr. Norman Vincent Peale after doing this.

All it takes is time. Don't waste it. You'll never know the difference you can make by Giving the Real Recognition Way.

Go Get'em Giving Ideas

1. Take time at the end of the day. Stop and think of someone you should send a thank you card to. Don't have any? Go out

and buy a supply and purchase some postage stamps while you are at it.

2. Take time after every interaction. This is for the advanced practitioners of giving people recognition. Stop to thank the person on the phone at the end of a conversation. Thank the server in a restaurant. Thank your spouse for the special things they do. Take time.

67.

IT'S ALL IN THE EXECUTION

The Principle of Execution is a critical piece to giving people Real Recognition™. If you blow this you will be making one of the worst recognition mistakes known to humankind.

Done correctly, your words and actions in giving the recognition will magnify its worth. Done improperly and you will diminish your recognition act to a fat zero.

Here are just a few simple steps to consider:

- Know the person's preferred name, not just their given name.
- Arrange for a good time of the work day to present or share the recognition so others can enjoy.
- Tell the person specifically what they did to merit the recognition… say it, and if needed, print it on a certificate.
- Orchestrate everything you can to create a memorable atmosphere and experience. Focus on right time, right place, and right environment.
- Know the person well enough to respect their wishes as to wanting public versus private acknowledgement.
- Tell the individual how their contribution made a difference to you, the client and the company.
- Have a camera or video-camera ready to capture the memory for the person.
- Invite people important to the recipient to be present to share in the experience.

Go Get'em Giving Ideas

1. Create a presentation checklist for yourself. Use this simply as a guide to help you make the recognition giving a great experience. Recognition is a managed experience.

2. Change the giving from a presentation to a celebration. It can be as simple as balloons, a personalized gift item, or having the right music playing. Your job is making positive perceptions that will linger and not be easily forgotten.

68.

MAKE IT PERSONAL

In doing some prep work and interviews for a client consultation, I have learned again the importance of being upfront and personal with recognition giving.

One of the feedback comments I have heard is the importance and sometimes lack of *personalizing* of the recognition being given to employees. This omission is a big mistake.

Personalizing is *everything* about making what you say, do, or give "personal" to the individual being acknowledged.

- Find out if the person wants public or private recognition – one person told me the recognition in their department is *always* private so no one else knows the good things going on.

- Template online certificates are good to aid the fast paced world we live in – simply customize them or add a personal, written note about the specific action achieved. Use the tools provided for recognition giving and make them personal.

- Walk about and truly get to know people – you and I are all overworked and have huge demands on our time, but the person who knows his or her people the best will get the best out of their people.

Go Get'em Giving Ideas

1. Personalizing can also mean inscribing their name on the item being given. Find unique items to give. Some specialty

chocolate stores will even ice on a name on a unique chocolate item. Make sure preferred name and spelling is right.

2. Getting to know the person is the real key to more effective personalization. Develop some type of a personal inventory to record facts and interests as you get to know your employee's likes, dreams and aspirations. Make their wishes come true.

69.

SLAP IN THE FACE

Imagine being in the HR department at Ford Motor Company in the U.S. and waking up the next morning to the headlines "Fired Ford worker says award like 'slap in the face.'" That would be a tough start to the work day.

The Associated Press on June 10, 2006 published this story so read on and see if you can figure out the recognition mistake that was made. Remember the angle of the story is strictly from the media's perspective. This could happen to any of us so be careful not to judge or jump to conclusions. Look at what reportedly happened and then we can step back together and look at some suggestions for you to consider.

Apparently, a 49-year old employee lost his job at Ford as a transmission engineering technician in January, just nine months shy of his 30-year anniversary, a milestone where he could retire with full benefits. He is suing the motor company because of the reduced pension and benefits he will receive in view of being let go before his anniversary.

The article stated how earlier in the month, the employee received a package from Ford with a certificate recognizing his years of service to Ford accompanied by a letter from then Ford Chairman and Chief Executive Bill Ford starting off with "Dear Fellow Employee."

Inside the package was also a set of plastic sizing rings for the employee to use and determine his ring size for a celebratory band to order along with a catalog from which to select a gift.

Can you just imagine how this guy was feeling?

So let's take a good look at this scenario, review each aspect of the situation carefully and provide some suggestions for consideration.

1. There appeared to be an automated years of service process without any apparent fail-safe human intervention.

Suggestion: When giving people recognition always check the individual's situation before proceeding and don't work solely from automated processes. Make the system a tool to work from.

2. The article does not mention any supervisory consultation that may or may not have occurred.

Suggestion: Consult with the immediate supervisor or manager of the employee or give prior e-mail notification of the forthcoming anniversary in advance of the date and then solicit feedback of any timing issues and situational concerns they are aware of.

3. The legal case of employee and employer would have been well known to HR department and managers.

Suggestion: Once a situation is identified meet face-to-face with the award recipient and acknowledge the emotions of the difficult situation. Invite an opportunity for the employee to still receive the appropriate honor for their years of service.

4. It does not appear from the story that he was spoken to ahead of time about his service award, and just received the customary package in the mail.

Suggestion: Solicit the employee's input on how to proceed and what choices they would like to make in view of the challenging circumstances. Respect their decision.

Go Get'em Giving Ideas

1. Review the story and check out your own recognition procedures and make any necessary course corrections. I have a quote on my office bulletin board from Ben Feldman from the insurance industry which states, "If you've got a problem make it a procedure and it won't be a problem anymore." This simple philosophy will answer many situational problems like the one shared here.

2. You can lose your head through execution! So be careful on *how* you give recognition and make sure there is always a human countercheck in all the automated processes that you might have.

70.

NOMINATIONS DON'T COUNT

Formal recognition is clearly a very measurable activity.

Where award processes require nomination steps then it is customary to measure the number of nominations made within a certain time period.

So the more nominations received in a given time period, the more successful and effective your formal recognition giving is doing. Right?

Well, not exactly. And herein lies a common mistake recognition practitioners seem to make.

Nominations are only one measure in the recognition equation.

Quick review: Measuring nominations submitted is purely a measure of the awareness, commitment and understanding of the recognition program by managers or staff. It shows how well the organization has communicated, promoted and reinforced the process. It shows the level of ease or difficulty in the actual submission process.

Where nominations do not count is when looking at measuring the actual effectiveness of formal recognition.

To measure the effectiveness and meaningfulness of formal awards and recognition programs you have to measure what employees and the award recipients think *not* the behaviors of those who submit nominations.

So you must ask employees and award recipients in order to measure and determine the recognition effectiveness. You could consider some of the following items:

- Was there an increase in the sense of pride the award generated?
- Was the award presented in a meaningful manner?
- Was the award given in a timely manner?
- How well did the manager do in presenting the award?
- Was there an increase in the number of employees attending the awards event?
- Did employee satisfaction and engagement scores improve (obviously not the only correlation)?
- How are our customer satisfaction scores doing?
- Did staff participation increase if open to all levels?
- Were improvement suggestions solicited from employees at each event?
- Were suggestions from previous awards events considered and implemented?

So be careful what it is you measure. That is why nominations alone as a measure don't count.

Go Get'em Giving Ideas

1. Measure right. A ruler is no good for measuring the temperature. Do a quick check and see what measuring sticks you are using to assess your recognition programs. One measure is good for certain behaviors and not for others. So define the behaviors and attitudes you want to measure and get both the ruler and the thermometer out.

2. Compare right. Yes, it is OK to benchmark against organizations but just remember their ideal body weight is not yours. So take other organizations numbers into consideration

but then at some point you have to disregard them and move with what is right for you. Establish your company's baseline performance measures, implement new behaviors and strategies, and then measure to compare the pre- and post-implementation measures of your program actions.

***

REAL RECOGNITION™ FOR REAL RESULTS!

You're invited to continue your education and development in effective recognition giving by becoming a subscriber to the monthly Real Recognition E-zine.

Keep the learning and ideas coming after you finish reading this book and make your employee recognition really last!

FREE! Subscription to the Real Recognition Ezine

Real Recognition Ezine is the electronic monthly magazine with proven recognition principles, strategies and techniques that produce real results. Discover my unique insights on practical recognition giving skills and new ideas for creating a culture to support appreciation, praise and recognition in the workplace.

In each issue you will receive latest research and advice on topics such as:
- Recognition Tips and Techniques
- Creating A Real Recognition™ Culture
- Non-monetary & Monetary/Tangible Recognition
- Helpful Recognition Resources
.... and much, much more!!

How can I subscribe to the "Real Recognition Ezine?"

Simply visit us online at **www.RealRecognition.com** and click on the subscribe button on the home page. Then follow the easy-to-follow subscribing instructions. Or just put SUBSCRIBE in the BODY of an e-mail and send it directly to us at: **info@RealRecognition.com**.

Subscriber privacy policy of confidentiality is strictly adhered to.

ABOUT ROY SAUNDERSON

Roy Saunderson is a leading North American expert on employee recognition. He is president and founder of the Recognition Management Institute, a consulting and training company specializing in showing leaders how to give "Real Recognition for Real Results."

A professional speaker for over 20 years, Roy founded the Recognition Management Institute over 12-years ago to address the difficulty managers have giving effective recognition to their employees. He has consulted and presented to clients across North America such as Bell Canada, Boeing, Ceridian, Disney Corporation, Johnson & Johnson, and 3M Canada as well as government departments and professional and trade associations. The Recognition Management Institute became a division of Rideau Recognition Solutions in 2005.

Roy is a judge for the Best Practices Awards for Recognition Professionals International, is a facilitator for their professional certification programs, and sits on their Education Committee. Roy is a member of Recognition Professionals International, Incentive Marketing Association, the International Federation for Professional Speakers, and the Canadian Association of Professional Speakers.

His overall message of "Real Recognition for Real Results" is built on solid principles and values, developing a clear articulated recognition strategy and in providing skills to get everyone caring and recognizing one another more effectively.

Roy has authored, "How to FOCUS on Success!" "101 Ways to Give EVERYDAY Real Recognition™," publishes the monthly Real Recognition E-zine, and has written numerous articles on employee recognition along with being a columnist with *HRO Today* magazine. He is currently writing additional books to assist senior leaders become more strategic with applying employee recognition and help practitioners in implementing recognition the right way.

To find out more about Roy Saunderson, *Real Recognition*™ products, consultation, and training services, and his availability to speak at your meeting, call 877-336-9601 or visit his website at www.RealRecognition.com.

NOTES

NOTES

NOTES